ARISTOTLE AND THE AMERICAN INDIANS

A Study in Race Prejudice in the Modern World

by

LEWIS HANKE

INDIANA UNIVERSITY PRESS
Bloomington & London

TO

CHARLES JULIAN BISHKO

AND

FRANCE V. SCHOLES

LONG TIME FRIENDS AND CO-WORKERS

IN HISPANIC HISTORICAL STUDIES

"*Every culture seems, as it advances toward maturity, to produce its own determining debate over the ideas that preoccupy it: salvation, the order of nature, money, power, sex, the machine and the like. The debate, indeed, may be said to be the culture, at least on its loftiest levels; for a culture achieves identity not so much through the ascendancy of one particular set of convictions as through the emergence of its peculiar and distinctive dialogue. . . . Intellectual history, properly conducted, exposes not only the dominant ideas of a period, or of a nation, but more importantly, the dominant clashes over ideas. Or to put it more austerely: the historian looks not only for the major terms of discourse, but also for major pairs of opposed terms which, by their very opposition, carry discourse forward. The historian looks, too, for the coloration or discoloration of ideas received from the sometimes bruising contact of opposites.*

"*As he does so and as he examines the personalities and biases of the men engaged in debate at any given historical movement, the historian is likely to discover that the development of the culture in question resembles a protracted and broadly ranging conversation: at best a dialogue—a dialogue which at times moves very close to drama.*"

R.W. B. Lewis, *The American Adam. Innocence, Tragedy and Tradition in the Nineteenth Century* (Chicago, 1955), pp. 1-2.

CONTENTS

		Page
INTRODUCTION	. . . .	ix
I. AMERICA AS FANTASY	. . . . .	1
II. ARISTOTLE AND AMERICA TO 1550	. . .	12
III. THE BATTLE BETWEEN LAS CASAS AND SEPÚLVEDA IS JOINED: 1547–1550	. . . . .	28
IV. THE GREAT DEBATE AT VALLADOLID, 1550–1551: THE SETTING	. . . . . .	38
V. THE GREAT DEBATE AT VALLADOLID, 1550–1551: THE APPLICATION OF ARISTOTLE'S THEORY OF NATURAL SLAVERY TO THE AMERICAN INDIAN	.	44
VI. THE GREAT DEBATE AT VALLADOLID, 1550–1551: THE WAGING OF JUST WAR AGAINST THE AMERICAN INDIAN	. . . . .	62
VII. AFTERMATH OF BATTLE, 1550–1955	. . .	74
(a) To the Basic Law of 1573	. . .	74
(b) Since 1573	. . . . .	88
VIII. "ALL THE PEOPLES OF THE WORLD ARE MEN"	.	96
APPENDIX A. The Exchange of Letters between Juan Ginés de Sepúlveda and Alfonso de Castro	. .	117
APPENDIX B. Materials Used to Prepare this Study	.	119
NOTES	. . . .	123
INDEX	. . . .	161

ILLUSTRATIONS

Bartolomé de Las Casas, Spanish Dominican and
Apostle to the American Indians . *Frontispiece*

Juan Ginés de Sepúlveda, Spanish Renaissance scholar
and Aristotelian . . . . . *page* 7

Indians in Puerto Rico experiment to find out whether
Spaniards are mortal 25

European conception of cruelties practised by American
Indians on Spaniards 32

First English translation of the Las Casas treatise
Brévissima relación de la destrucción de las Indias,
which denounces Spanish cruelty to the American
Indians 77

ABBREVIATIONS

Demócrates. Juan Ginés de Sepúlveda. Demócrates segundo o
de las justas causas de la guerra contra los indios. Tr. and
ed. by Ángel Losada. Madrid, 1951.

Documentos inéditos de América. Colección de documentos
inéditos relativos al descubrimiento, conquista, y coloni-
zación de las posesiones españolas en América y Oceania.
42 vols. Madrid, 1864–1884.

Las Casas. Bibliografía crítica. Bartolomé de Las Casas. Bibliografía crítica y cuerpo de materiales para el estudio de su
vida, escritos, actuación y polémicas que suscitaron
durante cuatro siglos. By Lewis Hanke and Manuel
Giménez Fernández. Santiago de Chile, 1954.

Introduction

WRITINGS on the Spanish conquest of America during recent years well illustrate the truth of the old maxim that a historian's work is never done and that the story of the past must be continually revised. Frequently this revision comes because of the discovery of new sources. At other times well-known materials yield a new interpretation. In the present study I have tried to use all available documents on the subject, including some hitherto unexploited manuscripts, and to examine all interpretations as a preliminary to setting forth my own view. And as "The Past is Prologue", or sometimes is, I have tried also to indicate how a struggle over ideas in 1550 is relevant to the present.

The influence of Aristotle's geographical conceptions on the discovery of America has long been known,[1] but it is only in recent years that the application of his doctrine of natural slavery to the American Indians during the Spanish conquest has been studied seriously. Generally speaking there was no true racial prejudice before the fifteenth century, for mankind was divided not so much into antagonistic races as into "Christians and infidels".[2] The expansion of Europe to Africa, America, and the East changed all this and thus the story of Spanish experience has a value for those who would understand race issues on the world scene.[3]

One of the most curious episodes in the intellectual history of the Western world occurred when two remarkable Spaniards—Bartolomé de las Casas and Juan Ginés de Sepúlveda—met in Valladolid in 1550 to debate this issue. Then for the first, and doubtless for the last, time a colonizing nation organized a formal enquiry into the justice of the methods used to extend its empire. For the first time, too, in the modern world we see an attempt to stigmatize a whole race as inferior, as born slaves according to the theory elaborated centuries before by Aristotle. The bitter dispute on this question, the influence exerted by the controversy on the policy of the Spanish crown in America, later applications of the doctrine to other peoples, and the significance of the sixteenth-century struggle for the world today form the substance of this essay.

I have received much help in its preparation. I would pay special tribute to those with whom I must disagree: Ángel Losada, Edmundo O'Gorman, and Robert E. Quirk. Each in his own way has stimulated me to re-examine my previous studies of the complicated story of the Valladolid disputation. In addition to my wife, others to whom I also owe a debt of gratitude are: R. Pierce Beaver, Charles Julian and Lucretia Bishko, Charles R. Boxer, Vicenta Cortés, José Cuellar, James Cummins, Ricardo Donoso, Alfonso García Gallo, Charles Gibson, Manuel Giménez Fernández, Otis Green, Peter S. Hanke, R. A. Humphreys, Javier Malagón, Garrett Mattingly, Gilbert McAllister, José de la Peña, Francis M. Rogers, John H. Rowe, France V. Scholes, Lotta M. and J. R. Spell, Frank M. Wardlaw, Wilcomb E. Washburn, and Schafer Williams. The Research Institute of the University of Texas provided funds for secretarial assistance, and Mrs. Ona Kay Stephenson typed well and faithfully several drafts.

It would be untrue to suggest that all or any of these persons completely approve the text of this book. They do not, nor is it to be expected that agreement can be reached on such a highly debatable event in history. Despite all the aid given me, this book remains for better or for worse my own responsibility.

Austin, Texas   Lewis Hanke
November, 1957

ARISTOTLE AND THE
AMERICAN INDIANS

I

America as Fantasy

At first sight the conjunction of Aristotle and the American Indians appears absurd and meaningless. One may ask why sixteenth-century Spaniards came to apply the ideas of a Greek, who lived four centuries before Christ, to the problems of their conquest of America. What did Aristotle say that had any relevance to the Indians? The explanation is simple. The opening up of a vast unknown world peopled by strange folk led the Spaniards as they advanced among them bearing the Cross to ask themselves who these people were. And in asking this, they found themselves involved in a larger question that Aristotle never had to face: How ought Christians to conduct themselves towards human beings who differ in colour, culture, and religion? Aristotle's authority remained so strong among Christian thinkers that some eminent Spaniards did not hesitate to apply his doctrine of natural slavery to the Indians. Others discovered that the experience and dogmas of the past were only partially helpful in attempting to answer the moral questions posed by the discovery of America.

Europe had, of course, accumulated some experience of relations with non-Christians during the slow frontier expansion of medieval times, which foreshadowed some of the events of the New World conquest.[1] Both the Spaniards and Portuguese passed through a long period of intimate contact with the more highly cultivated Arabs, who had a decisive influence on their way of life. The Jews also had played an important role in that process of peaceful cultural osmosis which distinguished certain periods of later Iberian medieval history. During the fifteenth century Spaniards had been confronted, in the course of their conquest of the Canary Islands, with peoples of different customs and different religion from their own. Indeed in these Islands disputes had developed on the justice of the treatment of the natives which suggest the sixteenth-century discussions in America.[2] And Portugal, as the great explorer of Africa, had brought to Europe a knowledge of far-off and strange peoples. But ordinarily the Portuguese enslaved without much compunction the natives they encountered, believing that any physical subjection suffered in the process was of minor importance compared with the great benefits derived from conversion.[3] In addition the Portuguese faced in Africa long-time geopolitical and religious enemies and waged war as a national crusade with full papal support.[4] It was the Spaniards who first realized the necessity to work out Christian laws to govern their relations with the Indians they encountered.

The peoples of Africa and Asia became known to Europe through the considerable body of travel literature popular at the end of the fifteenth century and in the early years of the sixteenth, when the printing press was becoming a power in the world and Spain's expansion was getting under way.[5] By contrast, America was at first of little interest to Europe, or so it would seem from the relative scarcity of publications on the newly-discovered lands. Throughout the sixteenth century Spanish literature and art reflected only faintly the stirring events occurring across the seas.[6] But as the impressive feats of Spanish arms brought Mexico and then Peru under Spanish rule, and as Spaniards from many walks of life went to take part in the conquest, the true significance of their new possessions gradually became better understood and by the middle of the sixteenth century the historian Francisco

López de Gómara characterized the discovery of America as the greatest event since the coming of Christ.[7]

The Spaniards who actually saw America not only became tremendously excited and stimulated but they tended to look at the New World through medieval spectacles.[8] The wealth of ideas and legends developed with such luxuriance during the Middle Ages was transferred at once to America; this medieval influence was especially marked during the early years of the discovery and conquest.[9] Columbus firmly asserted that he had discovered the terrestrial paradise, while others sought for the Fountain of Youth or tried to locate—in the general region of Nebraska and the Dakotas—the Seven Enchanted Cities which were believed to have been established by the seven Portuguese bishops who had fled there when the Arabs invaded the Iberian peninsula. The Admiral's head was full of medieval legends and allusions, for we also find him naming the Virgin Islands after St Ursula and her companions, the eleven thousand seagoing virgins.[10] Columbus also enquired after the monsters to be found on Hispaniola when he first landed there in 1493,[11] and Ferdinand Cortez sent back to the Emperor Charles V in 1522 not only considerable booty and a letter recounting the great deeds wrought in Mexico but also some samples of giants' bones found there.[12]

Spanish captains went forth to their conquest expecting to encounter many kinds of mythical beings and monsters depicted in medieval literature: giants, pygmies, dragons, griffins, white-haired boys, bearded ladies, human beings adorned with tails, headless creatures with eyes in their stomachs or breasts, and other fabulous folk. For a thousand years a great reservoir of curious ideas on man and semi-men had been forming in Europe, and was now freely drawn upon in America. St Augustine in his *City of God* had a whole chapter on "Whether the descendants of Adam or of the sons

of Noah produced monstrous races of men", and by the end
of the fifteenth century a rich body of fantastic ideas was
ready for use in America. Trumpet-blowing apes, for
example, "formed part of a loosely defined pictorial cycle
combining subjects from the world of fable with the exotic
beasts of the Bestiaries and the Marvels of the East".[13] It is not
surprising, therefore, to find that the early historian Gonzalo
Fernández de Oviedo had heard of a Peruvian monkey that
"was no less extraordinary than the griffins", for it had a long
tail, with the upper half of its body covered with many-hued
feathers and the lower half with smooth, reddish fur. It could
sing, "when it felt like it", in the same dulcet tones as a
nightingale or a lark.[14]

Wild men also had captured popular imagination during
the Middle Ages.[15] They were depicted on the façades of
churches, as decorations for manuscripts, and in tapestries, as
ferocious beings of wild mien rending lions barehanded or
smashing their skulls with trees or mighty clubs. Wild men
served as jamb figures on the façade of the fifteenth-century
San Gregorio monastery in Valladolid in which Las Casas
lived during the 1550 disputation with Sepúlveda.[16] The
wildman motif was much used in Spain, crossed the Atlantic
with Spanish workmen, and is seen on the façade of the Casa
del Montejo in Yucatan, built in 1549.[17] Wild men also supported the arms of Charles V in Tlaxcala.[18] Given this
medieval mélange of man, beast, and mythical creature, we
are not surprised to find that a 1498 edition of John of Holywood's *Sphaera Mundi* describes the inhabitants of the New
World as being "blue in colour and with square heads".[19]
One of the earliest pictures of American natives, printed as a
wood engraving about 1505, showed the same fantastic
spirit.[20] The caption read as follows:

"They go naked, both men and women; they have well-
shaped bodies, and in colour nearly red; they bore holes in

their cheeks, lips, noses and ears, and stuff these holes with blue stones, crystals, marble and alabaster, very fine and beautiful. This custom is followed alone by the men. They have no personal property, but all things are in common. They all live together without a king and without a government, and every one is his own master. They take for wives whom they first meet, and in all this they have no rule. They also war with each other, and without art or rule. And they eat one another, and those they slay are eaten, for human flesh is a common food. In the houses salted human flesh is hung up to dry. They live to be a hundred and fifty years old, and are seldom sick."[21]

Even more imaginative conceptions of the natives were held by some Spanish captains. Governor Diego Velázquez, despite his years of experience in Cuba, instructed Cortez to look for strange beings with great flat ears and others with dog-like faces whom he might expect to see in Aztec lands. Francisco de Orellana was so positive that he had encountered warrior women on his famous voyage of 1540 that the mightiest river in South America was named the Amazon. The Devil himself was to be found, some believed, on a certain island in the Caribbean Sea, but to balance this we find reports that the Apostle St James, patron saint of Spain, fought side by side with Spaniards in many of their military engagements in America.[22] Strange sea animals and assorted monsters of the deep sea were also to be expected on the trip across.[23] And, a more cheerful note, certain large birds found near Panama were reputed to sing together in a pleasing choral harmony.[24] The chronicler of Peru, Pedro Cieza de León, heard in 1550 that bones of giants had been found there and thought that giants might still exist in that vast territory which was still only partially conquered and imperfectly known.[25] El Dorado, that myth of easy gold, lured many a conquistador to his doom in the jungles and deserts of

America.[26] Gog and Magog were believed to be somewhere in the New World,[27] and even in the latter part of the sixteenth century a unicorn was reported seen in Florida.[28]

Fifteenth-century Europeans had assumed their knowledge of the world to be exact, and the appearance of a vast unknown continent across the seas shook their confidence in themselves. Ingenious attempts were made to demonstrate that the early Christian authorities foreshadowed that shattering event, the discovery of America.[29] If the new lands could be related somehow to the world they knew, a bridge could be built between the known and the unknown. The natives of this marvellous new world were, of course, at the centre of speculation. Even before the first decade had passed, these plumed and painted peoples—so inevitably and so erroneously called Indians—had become the principal mystery which perplexed the Spanish nation, conquistadores, ecclesiastics, crown, and common citizens alike. Who were they? Whence came they? What was their nature, their capacity for Christianity and European civilization? Most important of all, what relationship would be the right one for the Spaniards to establish with them?[30]

The popular image, in the first feverish months, of a terrestrial paradise was soon succeeded by that of a hostile continent peopled with armed warriors rushing out of the tropical forests or strange cities to resist the advance of the Spanish soldiers and the missionary efforts of their companion friars. The early suppositions that the lost Ten Tribes of Israel were the progenitors of the Indian—held by more than one serious writer of the day—or even the later idea that in some mysterious way the Welsh nation had sent out these strange shoots—failed to answer satisfactorily the urgent basic questions: Who and what are these creatures? How shall we treat them? Can they be Christianized and brought to a civilized way of life? How shall this be attempted, by war or by

JUAN GINES DE SEPÚLVEDA

Cordobes: Theólogo, crítico, filólogo, é Histo-
riador: nació en 1490. y murió
en 1573.

JUAN GINÉS DE SEPÚLVEDA, 1490–1573
SPANISH RENAISSANCE SCHOLAR AND ARISTOTELIAN

peaceful persuasion? The conquistadores tended to ask rather pointedly: When may just war be waged to compel the Indians to serve God and the king and us? And the ecclesiastics asked eagerly: How can the natives be made to change from what they are to what they ought to be?

Two circumstances were responsible for these questions, which were asked by no other European colonizing nation with such general and genuine concern. The first was the nature of the Spanish people themselves, a people legalistic, passionate, given to extremes, and fervently Catholic. Three events of the year 1492 reflect some of the most fundamental characteristics of Spaniards and their history. Granada, the last of the Moorish kingdoms, fell to the Catholic Kings Ferdinand and Isabella on January 2, the Jews were next expelled, and on August 3 Columbus set sail. The final conquest of Granada was the climax of a long national effort to establish Christian hegemony in Spain. This long travail had helped to prepare the nation for larger tasks. Isabella herself discovered this in that same year, 1492, when she bluntly asked the scholar Antonio de Nebrija, as he presented to her his Spanish *Gramática*, the first grammar of a European modern language ever written: "What is it for?", and the Bishop of Avila, speaking on behalf of the scholar, replied: "Your Majesty, language is the perfect instrument of empire."[31]

The second circumstance was the nature of the dominion exercised by the Spanish crown in America, by which the Spaniards felt themselves responsible for the conversion of the natives. The decrees of Pope Alexander VI, the famous bulls of donation of 1493, which were used at first to justify the exertion of Spanish power in the new lands, specifically entrusted to the crown of Castile the Christianization of these lands. Without becoming embroiled, as the Spaniards themselves became, in the legal and moral implications of these papal pronouncements, we may be clear that the Spaniards had, logically, to determine Indian nature and capacity before they could legitimately pursue either conquest or Christianization.

Most Spaniards, no matter what attitude they developed towards the Indians, were usually profoundly stirred by them. Kings and the Council of the Indies instituted prolonged and formal enquiries in both Spain and America on their nature. Few significant figures of the conquest failed to deliver themselves of opinions on the Indian's capacity for Christianity, ability to work, and general aptitude for European civilization. Among the documents which remain to us are not only opinions but also numerous and curious proposals for the protection and welfare of the Indians. Early in his career Las Casas proposed the introduction of Negro slaves to the islands, in order to spare Indians the heavy labour which was destroying them, but later repented and opposed Negro slavery as well as Indian slavery, "and for the same reasons".[32] Spaniards never fought, however, as hard or as consistently against Negro slavery as they did on behalf of the Indians, not even Las Casas. Despite his final rejection of Negro slavery, as late as 1544 he owned several Negro slaves and no document has come to light which reveals any concerted opposition to Negro slavery during the sixteenth century. Why did the consciences of Spaniards twinge more easily for Indians than for Negroes? Perhaps Iberian peoples had become accustomed to having Moslem Negro slaves, and Indians were not only new to them but had never had an opportunity to hear the faith before. The Jesuits Alonso de Sandoval and Pedro Claver were to work on behalf of Negroes in the seventeenth century but the moral conscience of the modern world was first roused by the plight of the American Indian.[33]

Many men and many methods were engaged in the attempt

to help the American Indians. In the same month (May, 1550) that saw the beginning of the famous discussion on the nature of the Indians, a Sevillan named Cristóbal Muñoz obtained a contract from the king to introduce 100 camels into Peru. Why? To spare the Indians the bearing of heavy burdens up and down the Andes.[34] The archives of Spain and America are full of absorbing documentation on what the conquerors thought of the conquered people in this first widespread meeting of races in modern times. The amount and quality of the information available is unparalleled in the records of any other colonizing nation, and constitutes a wealth of material not yet fully exploited by anthropologists.

As the conquerors and clerics moved forward into America in the uneasy partnership which the crown's double purpose of political dominion and religious conversion enjoined upon them, stubborn facts and theological convictions clashed resoundingly. The voices of individuals and of different factions—ecclesiastics, soldiers, colonists, and royal officials in America as well as of men of action and thought in Spain—rose continually during the sixteenth century in a loud chorus of conflicting advice to the Spanish kings and the Council of the Indies. Each man, each faction, held a profound conviction about the nature of the Indians and all generalized about them as though they were a single race. Each made his own views on the Indians the basis of a recommendation for a government policy which he urged upon the powers in Spain as the one true solution which would once and for all set the enterprise of the Indies on a firm and unassailable foundation. The crown considered all these recommendations and ruled above all individuals and all factions, jealous of its prerogatives and determined to prevent the growth of a powerful and turbulent aristocracy such as had just been broken in Spain by the unremitting efforts of Ferdinand and Isabella. It was the Emperor Charles V and his counsellors, therefore,

who had to decide eventually what doctrine should be applied
to the American Indians. In the feverish days of the early conquest, when even hard-bitten conquistadores suffered strange
dreams and the New World was to some men a place of
wonder and enchantment populated with mysterious and
bewildering people, it is not surprising that even the ancient
theory of Aristotle, that some men are born to be slaves, was
borrowed from antiquity and found conveniently applicable
to the Indians from the coasts of Florida to far-distant Chile.

II

Aristotle and America to 1550

THE discovery period is now considered one of the epochs of greatest intellectual activity in all history. As the Argentine philosopher, Francisco Romero, emphasizes, "there was developed during these years a new philosophy, a new vision of the cosmos, and a new science of nature".[1] The immensity and the natural phenomena of the new lands made a special impact on men's minds; Europeans discovered "more territory in seventy-five years than in the previous thousand years".[2] When the Portuguese carried home Negroes from Guinea it became obvious that the views of Strabo and Pliny must be revised, for these had stated that the equatorial zone was uninhabitable. Copernicus declared that his speculations on the sphericity of the earth were confirmed by the existence of islands discovered by the Portuguese.[3] The impact of the Spanish conquest of America was not limited to erudite circles; it was a popular movement, too, which permitted fantastic folk ideas to flourish as well as literary conceits. Some of the conquistadores were simple, others sophisticated, and many sprang from the lower strata of society. The voluminous records kept on passengers officially licensed to emigrate demonstrate that all manner and condition of men descended upon America, not merely well-to-do courtiers and nobles who presumably were possessed of the learning and literature of the age.[4]

Of all the ideas churned up during the early tumultuous years of American history, none had a more dramatic appli-

cation than the attempts made to apply to the natives there
the Aristotelian doctrine of natural slavery: that one part of
mankind is set aside by nature to be slaves in the service of
masters born for a life of virtue free of manual labour.
Learned authorities such as the Spanish jurist Juan Ginés de
Sepúlveda not only sustained this view with great tenacity
and erudition but also concluded that the Indians were in fact
such rude and brutal beings that war against them to make
possible their forcible Christianization was not only expedient
but lawful. Many ecclesiastics, including the noted Indian
apostle, the Dominican friar Bartolomé de Las Casas, opposed
this idea scornfully, with appeals to divine and natural law as
well as to their own experience in America. The controversy
became so heated and the king's conscience so troubled over
the question of how to carry on the conquest of the Indies in
a Christian way that Charles V actually suspended all expeditions to America while a junta of foremost theologians,
jurists and officials in the royal capital of Valladolid listened
to the arguments of Las Casas and Sepúlveda. All this
occurred in 1550, after Cortez had conquered Mexico,
Pizarro had shattered the Inca empire, and many other lesser-
known captains had carried the Spanish banners to far corners
of the New World.

The idea that someone else should do the hard manual
work of the world appealed strongly to sixteenth-century
Spaniards, who inherited a taste for martial glory and
religious conquest and a distaste for physical labour from
their medieval forefathers who had struggled for centuries to
free Spain from the Moslems. And when to this doctrine was
linked the concept that the inferior beings were also being
benefited through the labour they were performing for their
superiors, the proposition became invincibly attractive to the
governing class. The New World offered a rich field for the
bold and resourceful Spaniards who were prepared to fight

bravely and, if necessary, to die in the attempt to carve out a piece of empire for themselves and at the same time to advance Christianity and serve their king. They were not prepared, however, to settle down as farmers to till the soil or as miners to extract gold and silver from the bowels of the earth. That was work for Indians. When natives were not available, Spaniards complained to the king. The town fathers of Buenos Aires once informed the king that affairs were so bad there that Spaniards actually had to dig in the earth and plant crops if they were to eat. And once it was recorded by a Spaniard of ten years' experience in America that he had seen *hidalgos* die of hunger in Honduras in 1536, and other Spanish gentlemen sowing the fields "with their own hands", a scene he had never witnessed before.[5] At first some of the Spaniards mined gold themselves in the islands, but afterwards not even the rudest peasant would lift his hand, according to Las Casas.[6] Throughout the whole of the colonial period and in all lands colonized by Spain this same attitude prevailed. Juan de Delgado, writing in the middle of the eighteenth century about the Philippine Islands, records the identical reaction: "Do Spaniards work the soil and plant crops in these islands? Certainly not! On reaching Manila all become *caballeros*."[7] Here we see the extension to all Spaniards in the Indies of the concept of *caballero* held previously by only a favoured few at home—an idea that sometime a sociological historian will be able to develop with much amusing and curious detail.

A Scottish professor in Paris, John Major, was the first to apply to the Indians the Aristotelian doctrine of natural slavery. He also approved the idea that force should be used as a preliminary to the preaching of the faith, and published these convictions in a book in Paris in 1510.[8] In the next year, 1511, a Dominican friar named Antonio de Montesinos preached a revolutionary sermon in a straw-thatched church on the island of Hispaniola in the Caribbean. Speaking on the text "I am a voice crying in the wilderness", Montesinos delivered the first important protest against the treatment being accorded the Indians by his Spanish countrymen, enquiring: "Are these Indians not men? Do they not have rational souls? Are you not obliged to love them as you love yourselves?" This sermon in America led immediately to a dispute at Burgos in Spain from which issued the first two Spanish treatises on Indian problems and the first code drawn up for the treatment of Indians by Spaniards. It is worth noting that one of these treatises, by the friar Matías de Paz, entitled *Concerning the Rule of the Kings of Spain over the Indians*, is not only the first study of this question by a Dominican but also the first known statement that the American Indians are *not* slaves in the Aristotelian sense.

The laws of the Indies are usually cited to prove the kindly intentions of the Spanish monarchs towards the Indians, and this they do, but they also reveal other important matters.[9] The Laws of Burgos, promulgated in 1512, not only included regulations on the labour of the Indians, their Christianization, and the food, clothes, and beds to be supplied to them, but also stipulated significantly in law number 24 that "no one may beat or whip or call an Indian dog (*perro*) or any other name unless it is his proper name". A Latin American scholar once insisted that calling an Indian a "dog" in those days was much like an American college student's affectionate name-calling of a fraternity brother. One may suspect, nevertheless, that the law faithfully reflects the contemptuous attitude towards Indians of many Spaniards during those early, turbulent days, and that the epithet was the adaptation for America of the "*perro moro*" vituperative phrase commonly applied in Spain to Moslems.

A further question, how to make certain that conquests proceeded according to just and Christian principles, was raised in 1513 and resulted in the adoption of the famous juridical declaration known as the Requirement, which had to be read formally to the Indians before the conquistadores could legally launch hostilities.[10] This manifesto makes curious reading today. It begins with a brief history of the world since its creation and an account of the establishment of the papacy, which leads naturally to a description of the donation by Alexander VI of "these isles and Tierra Firme" to the kings of Spain. The Indians are required to acknowledge their overlordship and to allow the faith to be preached to them. If they comply, well and good. If they do not, the Requirement lists the punitive steps the Spaniards will take forthwith. They will enter the land with fire and sword, will subjugate the inhabitants by force, and, to quote this document, which was read to many a startled Indian in a language he did not understand: "We shall take you and your wives and your children, and shall make slaves of them, and as such shall sell and dispose of them, as their Highnesses may command; and we shall take away your goods, and shall do all the harm and damage that we can, as to vassals that do not obey."

The first specific American application of the Aristotelian doctrine of natural slavery occurred in 1519 when Juan Quevedo, bishop of Darien, and Las Casas clashed at Barcelona before the young Emperor Charles V. Aristotle had not been used to justify slavery in medieval Spain, so that Las Casas was treading on unknown ground. But he marched ahead and denounced both Quevedo and Aristotle, whom he described as a "gentile burning in Hell, whose doctrine we do not need to follow except in so far as it conforms with Christian truth".[11] When Las Casas made this outburst against Aristotle he was a mature man over forty-five years old, one of the old-timers in America, who had been converted to the cause of the Indians five years previously. But he had not been subjected to the discipline and instruction of the Dominican Order, which he was to enter in 1522 during a period of deep dejection after the failure of his plan to colonize Tierra Firme with God-fearing, honest labourers who would help and not oppress the Indians.

Anti-Aristotelians there were in Spain, but in 1519 Las Casas was arguing from his heart rather than his head. He was fresh from the Caribbean Islands and had come to protest against the royal approval given to bringing Indians from other islands to work in the mines and on the farms of Hispaniola. Due to the "wrong" advice of the council, the king had signed the orders, "just as if rational men were pieces of wood that could be cut off trees and transported for building purposes, or like flocks of sheep or any other kind of animals that could be moved around indiscriminately, and if some of them should die on the road little would be lost". On the contrary, insisted Las Casas, the Indians were rational men, "not demented or mistakes of nature, nor lacking in sufficient reason to govern themselves", as he had proved in a treatise.

In this first clash with Aristotelian ideas, Las Casas enunciated the basic concept which was to guide all his action on behalf of the Indians during the remaining almost half century of his passionate life: "Our Christian relation is suitable for and may be adapted to all the nations of the world, and all alike may receive it; and no one may be deprived of his liberty, nor may he be enslaved on the excuse that he is a natural slave, as it would appear that the reverend bishop [of Darien] advocates".

Later at Valladolid Las Casas was to be more respectful of Aristotle, who was after all the dominant philosopher in Renaissance times and whose ideas had prepared the philosophical substratum of Catholicism. But even in this first brush with the doctrine of constituted authority Las Casas demonstrated the independent nature of his thinking. He did not support slavery, though St Augustine had sanctioned it and indeed had held that it was not only no impediment to virtue but afforded a unique opportunity for the practice of certain virtues such as humility, forgiveness, modesty, obedience, and patience.[12] Las Casas in 1519 at Barcelona rejected the dominant view towards slavery in the Middle Ages that inequalities and injustices were to be accepted as part of God's programme for the regeneration of the human race.[13] Nothing that he learned or saw in the years intervening between the disputes in 1519 and 1550 caused him to alter his fundamental thesis that the enslavement of the American Indians was wrong, and that the strongest supports for his doctrine were the Christian Church and God himself. This early Barcelona dispute appears to have had little influence, however, on the course of the battle over Indian character, which continued to agitate Spaniards.

Early in the conquest Spaniards attempted to distinguish between the fierce and supposedly cannibalistic Caribs and other Indians. If judged to be Caribs, the natives could be warred against unmercifully and justly enslaved. The manuscript material on this subject awaiting the historian-anthropologist is extensive[14] and needs to be studied, for it now appears that while some Caribs did eat human flesh, sixteenth-century slave raiders were inclined to apply the term "Carib" rather loosely. The Indians along the tropic shores of the Caribbean became greatly agitated when they saw Spaniards approaching with a notary public ready to take down declarations that they were eaters of human flesh, and one instance was recorded of Indians killing friars because they had given a Spanish captain a piece of paper which the Indians believed to be a formal declaration of Indian cannibalism. Later Fray Fernando de Carmellones informed the Council of the Indies, in a pungent letter on the conversion and treatment of the Indians, that "if anyone says he has seen the Indians eat friars, the Council should consider it a joke".[15] Juan de Castellanos, the sixteenth-century poet, declared that the Caribs were given this name, not because they were cannibals, but because they stoutly defended their homes.

Indians other than Caribs, however, were the subject of most of the disputes. Juan de Zumárraga, Franciscan and bishop of Mexico, played a notable role in this conflict of ideas simply by believing that the Indians were rational beings whose souls could be saved.[16] Every one of his contributions to Mexican culture was based on this conviction: the establishment of the famous *colegio* for boys at Tlatelolco and the school for Indian girls in Mexico City, the bringing of the first printing press to America, the movement for a university in Mexico, and the writing of books for Indians. An indication of the bitter and open conflict that raged on the subject in 1537, the year after Zumárraga established the school for Indians at Tlatelolco, is the fact that Pope Paul III found it necessary to issue the famous bull *Sublimis Deus* in which he stated that Indians were not to be treated as "dumb brutes created for our service" but "as truly men . . . , capable of understanding the Catholic faith". And the pope ordered: "The said Indians and all other people who may later be discovered by Christians, are by no means to be deprived of their liberty or the possession of their property, even though they may be outside the faith of Jesus Christ . . . nor should they in any way be enslaved".[17]

Las Casas manifested the same spirit as his life-long friend Zumárraga when he insisted on having the Indians adequately instructed in the rudiments of the faith before baptism. In an emergency, as for example when Indian children in Cuba had been disembowelled by Spanish soldiers, Las Casas was willing to baptize them without instruction before they died.[18] Under normal circumstances, he insisted Indians understand the faith before accepting it. Other missionaries in those early days, particularly Franciscans, placed no such emphasis on a thorough education, believed in mass baptism, and sprinkled holy water over Indian heads until their strength failed. They rang up impressive baptismal statistics, and calculated that they had thus saved over four million souls in Mexico alone from 1524 to 1536.[19] The record was established in Xochimilco where two Franciscans baptized 15,000 Indians in a single day. Such persons were impatient with Las Casas, who wanted to make certain that each Indian was properly instructed in the faith before baptism. Some friars were impatient with the Indians, too, for their slowness in learning the catechism. One of the first missionaries in Mexico, the Franciscan Martín de Valencia, beat Indians to hasten the process of their learning, never seemed satisfied with the ability of the Indians, and shortly before his death in 1531 planned to sail from the Isthmus of Tehuantepec for lands across the Pacific where he hoped to find men of "great capacity"[20]—perhaps he was thinking of the tales told by medieval travellers to the court of the Great Khan and other wondrous places of the East.

In general, however, the friars went about their missionary activities with uplifted hearts and a firm conviction that the souls of the Indians constituted the true silver to be mined in the Indies. There was no time to be lost, for the discovery and conquest not only afforded an opportunity to bring the Gospel to the Indians but also foreshadowed the rapid approach of the end of the world and the coming of the millennial kingdom.[21] Vasco de Quiroga was convinced that the Indians still lived in the Golden Age, while Europeans had decayed.[22] Though the Church was being destroyed in Europe, or at least challenged by Luther, the friars determined that a new and more powerful Church should be built in America. One Dominican with even more exalted ideas came to believe that the Church was finished in Europe, that the Indians were the elect of God, and that their new world Church would last for a thousand years.[23]

Baptismal struggles continued, however, on American soil. Not only were questions raised by Dominicans and Augustinians about the baptismal methods of the Franciscans, but the question arose whether friars had a right to baptize at all. An unpublished edict of Pope Paul III, dated February 21, 1539, would seem to indicate that even some Franciscans felt scruples on this point, for they arranged to have their protector in Rome, Cardinal Francisco de Quiñones, obtain authorization for them to perform the baptismal ceremony.[24]

Las Casas in 1546 created a painful scene in the Franciscan monastery at Tlaxcala when Fray Toribio de Benavente, known as Motolinía, asked him to baptize an Indian—since existing regulations prohibited Motolinía from doing so. The Indian had travelled a long distance to be baptized and Las Casas robed himself to perform the ceremony. Discovering that the Indian was unprepared, he refused to proceed, to the great annoyance of Motolinía, who neither forgot nor forgave.[25] And Las Casas long remembered Motolinía's attitudes and doctrines, for the Franciscan believed that the faith should be preached quickly, "if necessary by force".[26] This idea was revolting to Las Casas, who is supposed to have used his influence to keep Motolinía from getting a bishopric, an action which permanently embittered the Franciscan.[27]

Ironically enough, in many other important respects Las Casas and Motolinía thought alike on Indian affairs. The Franciscan missionary praised highly the ability of the Indians to learn Spanish, Latin and "all the sciences, arts, and crafts that they have been taught". A chapter of his *History of the Indians of New Spain* is devoted to "The Good Talent and Great Ability of the Indians". They were particularly apt in music, and an Indian singer in Tlaxcala composed an entire

Mass that had been approved by experienced Castilian musicians. In one month an Indian youth in Tehuacán had taught others to perform acceptably in Masses, vespers, hymns, motets, and the *Magnificat*.[28] Motolinía also denounced the Spaniards' cruelty to the Indians in a bitter and wholesale fashion which reminds one of the fulminations of Las Casas. He charged that "countless" natives were killed in labour at the mines, that service at Oaxaca was so destructive that for half a league around it one could not walk except on dead bodies or bones, and that so many birds flocked there to scavenge that they darkened the sky.[29] Only he who could count the drops of water in a rainstorm or the grains of sand in the sea could count the dead Indians in the ruined lands of the Caribbean Islands, cried Motolinía.[30] Las Casas himself made no more compelling statement than this. But he had evidently come to feel that Motolinía's views on baptism were unsound, and so these two outstanding friars of the conquest period were not friends, but enemies.

Disputes over baptism increased in number and intensity as the conquest proceeded. Las Casas opposed easy baptism so strenuously that the quarrel was taken from Mexico across the ocean to Spain for resolution. Charles V decided to refer the issue to the Dominican Francisco de Vitoria and a group of other notable theologians at the University of Salamanca, who in 1541 supported unanimously the view that Indians should indeed be instructed before baptism.[31] Vitoria, in his famous lectures at Salamanca which showed him to be one of the soaring thinkers of the century, also defended the Indians from the charge of irrationality.[32] There must have been a number who applied Aristotle's doctrine of natural slavery to the Indians, for Vitoria in *De Indis* analysed and refuted it long before Sepúlveda espoused it.[33] "The Indian aborigines . . . are not of unsound mind," asserted Vitoria, "but have, according to their kind, the use of reason. This is clear, because there is a certain method in their affairs; they have polities which are carefully arranged and they have definite marriage and magistrates, overlords, laws, and workshops, and a system of exchange, all of which call for the use of reason; they also have a kind of religion."[34]

Ideas are hard to kill by university pronouncements, however, or even with papal bulls. Thus the Dominican Juan Ferrer was reported to have prepared and sent to Pope Paul III a treatise on Mexican archaeology designed to dispel, once and for all, persistent doubts of the Indians' rationality by describing their architectural remains, their language and literature, and the vivid hieroglyphic depiction of their history.[35] Domingo de Santo Tomás announced, for example, in the prologue to his *Gramática, o arte de la lengua general de los indios del Perú* that his principal intention was to demonstrate, by his account of the beauties and subtleties of their language, the falsity of the idea that the Peruvian Indians were barbarians.[36]

In 1549 another Dominican friar, Domingo de Betanzos, who had been a missionary in America for many years, exemplified the Spanish preoccupation with Indian nature. As an old man, Betanzos wavered in his earlier conviction that the Indians were as incapable as children and ought never to be raised to the priesthood. Some years before he had applied the term *bestias* to them in a written memorial presented to the Council of the Indies. Now on his deathbed in Valladolid, just a year before Las Casas and Sepúlveda were to wrangle in the same city over the question whether the Indians were natural slaves, Betanzos swore before a notary that he had erred in his remarks about the Indians "through not knowing their language or because of some other ignorance" and formally abjured the statements in the memorial.[37] Some students today assert that Betanzos and others who spoke harshly about the Indians did not mean that they were really "beasts" in the true and full philosophic sense of the word, and this may be true, though it is impossible to know now exactly what they meant.[38] It seems clear, however, that some Spaniards—even ecclesiastics— held an extremely low opinion of the character and capacity of the Indians for whose salvation they had left their homes and travelled thousands of miles. And it is certain that the question of the true nature of the Indians agitated and baffled many Spaniards throughout the sixteenth century, and that it became a prime issue of the Spanish conquest which divided and embittered conquistadores, ecclesiastics, and administrators alike.

How different was the attitude of Zumárraga from that of his confessor Betanzos! In Zumárraga's eyes, the Indians were poor and ignorant, but that was no reason for avoiding or depreciating them. A homely illustration of this may be seen in the encounter between Zumárraga and certain secular Spaniards in Mexico who urged him to have less to do with the filthy and poorly-clad Indians. "Your Reverend Lordship is no longer young or robust, but old and infirm," they warned him, "and your constant mingling with the Indians may bring you great harm." Whereupon the bishop indignantly replied: "You are the ones who give out an evil smell according to my way of thinking, and you are the ones who are repulsive and disgusting to me, because you seek only vain frivolities and lead soft lives just as though you were not Christians. These poor Indians have a heavenly odour to me; they comfort me and give me health, for they exemplify for me that harshness of life and penitence which I must espouse if I am to be saved."[39]

What the Indians thought of their conquerors, on the other hand, can only be surmised from stray bits of evidence. In 1508 Puerto Rican Indians decided to determine whether Spaniards were mortal or not, by holding them under water

INDIANS IN
PUERTO RICO
EXPERIMENT TO
FIND OUT WHETHER
SPANIARDS ARE
MORTAL

(According to
Theodore de Bry)

to see whether they could be drowned.[40] The Dutch artist Theodore de Bry depicted this remarkable experiment, as well as scenes of Indians hanging themselves or taking poison in acts of mass suicide caused by the profound shock they had suffered at the overthrow of their culture. Spanish colonists reported that the terror inspired by the notorious Nuño de Guzmán was so great in Mexico about 1530 that Indians desisted from relations with their wives, because their children would only be doomed to slavery.[41] The later, gossipy Girolamo Benzoni reported that an aged chief in Nicaragua, Don Gonzalo, asked him: "What is a Christian, what are Christians? They ask for maize, for honey, for cotton, for women, for gold, for silver; Christians will not work, they are liars, gamblers, perverse, and they swear."[42] In Peru Benzoni wrote that Spaniards committed such cruelties that the Indians "not only would never believe us to be Christians and children of God, as boasted, but not even that we were born on this earth or generated by a man and born of a woman; so fierce an animal, they concluded, must be the offspring of the sea".[43] How representative these Indian opinions were we shall never know. The history of the Spanish conquest was written, in large part, by the conquerors alone.

Whether Spaniards praised or depreciated the ability and achievements of the Indians, however, they were certain that the natives would be improved by being Christianized. No incident has been found in America to match the experience of certain nineteenth-century Russian priests who discovered a tribe on the islands of the Bering Sea leading a life so nearly in accord with the Gospel of Christ that the missionaries confessed they had better be left alone.[44] No Spaniards doubted the Indians' need of the Christian message, though they might disagree heartily with each other on how it ought to be delivered. Not only was there an important group determined to Christianize the Indians by peaceful persuasion, but some bold Spaniards denounced the cruelty of their countrymen. Domingo de Santo Tomás in Lima protested the Council of the Indies in a powerful indictment dated July 1, 1550, that Indians in Peru were being treated inhumanly "as though they were brute animals (*animales brutos*) and even worse than asses".[45]

It was just a month later that Sepúlveda invoked the authority of Aristotle in Valladolid to stigmatize all the Indians of the New World as natural slaves. This was no casual or jocose description of the Indians as "dogs", which had been prohibited by the Laws of Burgos in 1512. It was a far more sweeping charge and it led to the last great dispute on Indian affairs in Spain. Coming presently to consider in detail the 1550 disputation of Las Casas and Sepúlveda at Valladolid against the background of events leading up to it, we shall see how inevitably this great debate on the nature of the American Indians actually grappled with the complicated problem of Spanish rule in America.

III

The Battle between Las Casas and Sepúlveda is Joined, 1547-1550

LAS CASAS could be in Valladolid in 1550 to confront Sepúlveda because he had returned to Spain for the last time in 1547 at the age of seventy-three after almost half a century of experience in Indian affairs, climaxed by his services as bishop of Chiapa in southern Mexico.[1] There he had infuriated his parishioners who held Indians and enjoyed service and tribute from them under the encomienda system, by insisting that Spaniards holding Indians could be confessed only according to certain strict regulations which he himself had drawn up. When this *Confesionario* was enforced rigidly, few encomenderos could be granted absolution. Tomás López, a royal official sent to Chiapa to punish those who had mistreated the Dominicans during Las Casas' period as bishop, found that some Spaniards had not confessed for five or six years and that others had died pleading in vain for the last rites of the Church.[2] In retaliation, encomenderos brought pressure to bear on Indians not to provide friars with food or to work on building monasteries, and at times threatened the Dominicans with physical violence.[3]

During his last months in America Las Casas had also, characteristically, been engaged in acrimonious discussion concerning his large treatise entitled *The Only Way of Attracting All People to the True Religion*. The method he proposed was peaceful persuasion; one of his principal objectives in going in 1544 at an advanced age to the poor and relatively unimportant bishopric of Chiapa had been to lend his influential support to the current attempts of his brother Dominicans to preach the faith in the province of True Peace without the use of any force whatsoever. This attempt, the last great enterprise which engaged his attention in America, embodied what was in many respects his most important concept of the proper relationship between Spaniards and Indians. Indians must be Christianized by peaceful means alone, he insisted, with no soldiers, no force, only the persuasion of the Gospel preached by godly men. Just before leaving America for the last time, Las Casas participated in a turbulent meeting in Mexico City on the nature of Spanish rule in which he condemned war against the Indians, whether to convert them or to remove obstacles to missionaries preaching the faith, as "perverse, unjust, and tyrannical".[4]

During his last year as bishop in America, Las Casas learned with horror that some of the famous New Laws for which he had struggled so mightily in 1542 had been revoked. The encomienda system, which the New Laws would eventually have abolished, was to be allowed to continue after all and the encomenderos were now emboldened to begin a vigorous campaign to make these grants perpetual, with civil and criminal jurisdiction over the Indians added if possible. The struggle over *perpetuidad* now overshadowed most other Indian problems.

When Las Casas reached Spain in 1547, therefore, he began organizing for the battle. We find the Indians of Oaxaca in Mexico giving him and his constant companion Friar Rodrigo de Andrada legal authority to represent them before the Council of the Indies,[5] and the Indians in Chiapa did likewise.[6] Later, in Peru, Domingo de Santo Tomás organized the Indians there to authorize Las Casas to offer Philip II a large sum of money to deny perpetuity. It was in fact a blank cheque, for Las Casas was to offer more cash than the encomenderos, no matter how high their bid for the privilege of perpetuidad. Manoeuvres such as these have led historians to emphasize Las Casas' qualities as a politician.[7]

His powerful influence at court was recognized at this time, for we find the Viceroy of New Spain Luis de Velasco asking Las Casas to help him get his salary increased.[8] Persons who had a candidate to suggest as a possible viceroy also wrote to Las Casas,[9] and Balthasar Guerra of Chiapa found that the concession of an encomienda to his natural son Juan was annulled by the crown because Las Casas said that his Indians had been treated unjustly.[10] The veteran friar is described in these years in royal orders as being "old and worn out" but he never slackened his stern and passionate pace.[11] His zeal in recruiting hardworking and dedicated missionaries continued unabated, and it is clear from the number of royal orders he inspired and the number of projects he initiated during the five years after his final return to Spain in 1547 that this was the most intensely productive and agitated period of his life. It was then, too, that he put into shape the treatises printed at Sevilla in 1552 and 1553, by which his ideas have become known to the world.

The most dramatic and important episode of this period, however, was his dispute with Juan Ginés de Sepúlveda, who had composed a treatise which sought to prove that wars against Indians were just and even constituted a necessary preliminary to their Christianization. The manuscript had been written under the high auspices of the President of the Council of the Indies, who encouraged Sepúlveda to write the book, assuring him that "it would be a service to God and the King". Sepúlveda had set to work at once; in a few days a manuscript version of the treatise was being circulated at court and, according to his own account, was approved by all who read it. When the manuscript was rejected by the

Council of the Indies, Las Casas stated that Sepúlveda prevailed upon friends at court to have the hearing transferred to the Council of Castile which, according to Las Casas, "was entirely ignorant of affairs of the Indies". It was at this moment that Las Casas arrived from Mexico, understood the gravity of the situation, and raised such an outcry that the Council of Castile hastened to refer the thorny matter to the universities of Alcalá and Salamanca, where it was discussed during the spring and early summer of 1548. After "many and very critical disputes," states Las Casas, "the university authorities determined that the treatise should not be printed, for its doctrine was not sound."

Las Casas was not alone in his opposition to Sepúlveda's doctrine.[12] As early as 1546 Melchor Cano had written against it in a learned commentary, and in 1549 Alonso de Maldonado supported Las Casas in a petition to the king.[13] But it was the aged bishop who led those who condemned Sepúlveda's views and acted as public prosecutor against them.

It was a bold step for Las Casas to engage such a scholar as Sepúlveda in learned combat, for this humanist who stepped forward to give comfort to Spanish officials and conquistadores possessed one of the best trained minds of his time, supported his views with many learned references, and enjoyed great prestige at court. Sepúlveda during his twenty years in Italy had become one of the principal scholars in the recovery of the "true" Aristotle.[14] His contributions to learning were recognized in Spain, and on the eve of the battle with Las Casas he had just completed and published at Paris in 1548 his Latin translation of Aristotle's *Politics*, which he considered his principal contribution to knowledge. It was the best translation that had appeared, and was recognized for centuries as an indispensable work.[15] Therefore when Sepúlveda began to write on America he was completely saturated

EUROPEAN
CONCEPTION
OF CRUELTIES
PRACTISED BY
AMERICAN
INDIANS
ON SPANIARDS

(According to
Theodore de Bry)

with the theory of "The Philosopher", including his much-discussed concept that certain men are slaves by nature.

While Sepúlveda pressed the authorities to approve his treatise which pronounced the wars against the Indians just, Las Casas was vehemently arguing that they were, on the contrary, scandalously unjust and that all conquests must stop if the royal conscience was to be kept unsullied. His formula was precisely what it had been for years: convert the Indians by peaceful means alone and they will afterwards become faithful Spanish subjects. Las Casas not only preached this doctrine, he also had striven mightily to put it into practice in Chiapa. Though his achievements in this field may have been exaggerated, the accomplishments of the Dominicans in preaching the faith there were considerable. The story of the victory achieved by diplomacy and prudence has not yet been fully told, and may never be. A sort of Hollywood version involving conversion by music and poetry, the fortunate marriage of a cacique, and other romantic touches was given in the early seventeenth century by the Dominican chronicler Antonio de Remesal.[16] Curiously enough Las Casas' reputation now seems to suffer on account of these hagiographical embellishments of his admirer, though he never claimed any of the marvellous achievements described by Remesal.[17]

The truth was much more prosaic, though sufficiently wonderful. Despite the active doubt and constant harassment of nearby secular Spaniards, the work of peaceful persuasion went on, strongly backed by the court which was steadily influenced by Las Casas to support the pious enterprise with floods of royal orders on its behalf. During the period of sparring with Sepúlveda, for example, Las Casas, in addition to all his other activities, busied himself with inducing the king to despatch encouraging messages to the Dominicans on the battle-line in Chiapa, which assured them of his appreciation for their notable labours in converting the Indians, commended them for their patience under provocations by the Spaniards, and requested more information on their efforts so that proper rewards could be made.[18]

Las Casas' principal efforts in the years immediately before the Valladolid dispute, however, were devoted to stopping what he declared to be oppression of the Indians and unjust wars against them. Conditions in the New World were not propitious. Pedro de la Gasca had put down a serious revolt in Peru, and Spaniards there were in no mood to listen to arguments in favour of a peaceful approach to Indian affairs. The unfortunate first viceroy to Peru, Blasco Núñez de Vela, had tried to enforce the New Laws in favour of the Indians in that violent land. He was captured by the angry and independent conquistadores, who showed their disrespect for royal authority by not only killing the viceroy but by nonchalantly carrying his head about suspended by a string.[19] The discreet and able royal representative, La Gasca, had brought peace and re-established the king's authority—though without wholeheartedly enforcing the doctrines of Las Casas.

We know what the state of mind of Las Casas was at this moment, thanks to Marcel Bataillon's recent discovery in the Archive of the Indies of a letter written by Las Casas to an unnamed correspondent, possibly Domingo de Soto the confessor of Charles V.[20] Las Casas, in a desperate effort to convince someone close to the Emperor that the conquests in America must be halted and all Indians incorporated under the crown, was answering previous objections made by his correspondent that the New World was far away and that even pious missionaries offered conflicting advice on the proper action to be taken. Las Casas bitterly reproached the Franciscans and Mercedarians who had supported the conquistadores, and praised the dramatic action of one of the oldest Franciscans in Mexico, probably Francisco de Soto, who had reversed his original decision and had eaten the paper on which he had previously signed his name supporting perpetuity of encomiendas. The ink has faded on this newly-found Las Casas document and the handwriting is abominable but the letter, full of corrections and blottings, written on the back of another one over four centuries ago, still conveys the conviction and eloquence of Las Casas. "Wherever else in the world", he asked, "have rational men in happy and populous lands been subjugated by such cruel and unjust wars called conquests, and then been divided up by the same cruel butchers and tyrannical robbers as though they were inanimate things, have been enslaved in an infernal way, worse than in Pharaoh's day, treated like cattle being weighed in the meat market and, God save the mark, are looked upon as of less worth than bedbugs? How can the words of those who support such iniquities be believed?"[21] Las Casas energetically affirmed that the necessary reforms could be achieved, if only the necessary laws were made by the Council of the Indies and upright men appointed to execute them in America. He recommended one bishop who would be excellent for the work, and advised that another person under no circumstances be allowed to go. Here we see Las Casas the lobbyist at work. And as always this practical and realistic apostle stressed that the arrangements he proposed would not only redound to the benefit of the Indians and to the increase of Christianity, but also to the "incomparable temporal interests" of the king.[22]

In the closing paragraphs of his letter, Las Casas urged that further action be not delayed until La Gasca returned from Peru, as his correspondent had evidently suggested. Some good decisions had recently been taken by the Council of the Indies and more were required. Here Las Casas probably referred to Council approval of his own breath-taking proposal, which made conquistadores up and down the Indies grind their teeth in rage, that the licences of all expeditions then under way be revoked and that no similar grants be made in the future. A drastic step in this direction was actually taken by the Council of the Indies on July 3, 1549, when it advised the king that the dangers both to the Indians and to the king's conscience which the conquests incurred were so great that no new expedition ought to be licensed without his express permission and that of the Council. Moreover, concluded the Council, a meeting of theologians and jurists was needed to discuss "how conquests may be conducted justly and with security of conscience". This statement by the highest board in Spain on Indian affairs is worth quoting. The Council stated that, although laws had of course been issued previously to regulate the conquests, "we feel certain that these laws have not been obeyed, because those who conduct these conquests are not accompanied by persons who will restrain them and accuse them when they do evil.

"The greed of those who undertake conquests and the timidity and humility of the Indians is such that we are not certain whether any instruction will be obeyed. It would be fitting for Your Majesty to order a meeting of learned men, theologians, and jurists, with others according to your pleasure, to discuss and consider concerning the manner in which these conquests should be carried on in order that they may be made justly and with security of conscience. An instruction for this purpose should be drawn up, taking into account all that may be necessary for this, and should be considered a law to govern henceforth the conquests approved by this Council as well as those approved by the Audiencias."[23]

The king now took the final step and ordered on April 16, 1550, that all conquests be suspended in the New World until a special group of theologians and counsellors should decide upon a just method of conducting them. Las Casas had won his point; the machinery of conquest was ordered to stop short. Both Sepúlveda and Las Casas agreed that there should be a meeting, and this, too, was decreed by the king and Council of the Indies to take place in 1550, the very year in which Américo Castro states that "the Spaniard had attained a zenith of glory".[24] Probably never before or since has a mighty emperor—and in 1550 Charles V, Holy Roman Emperor, was the strongest ruler in Europe with a great overseas empire besides—ordered his conquests to cease until it was decided if they were just.

This was the background against which Sepúlveda and Las Casas began their discussions in Valladolid on the justice of wars waged in far-off America and on the application of Aristotelian doctrine to the Indians.

The Great Debate at Valladolid, 1550-1551: The Setting

THE sessions began in mid-August, 1550, and continued for about a month before the "Council of the Fourteen", summoned by Charles V to sit in Valladolid.[1] Among the judges were such outstanding theologians as Domingo de Soto, Melchor Cano, and Bernardino de Arévalo, as well as veteran members of the Council of Castile and of the Council of the Indies, and such experienced officials as Gregorio López, the glossator of the well-known edition of the Spanish law code known as the *Siete Partidas*. Unfortunately, the great Dominican Francisco de Vitoria, considered by many the most able theologian of the century, had died in 1546. Had he lived, the Emperor might well have named him a member of the group and another classic work from his pen might have resulted. We might also know whether Las Casas or Sepúlveda more faithfully followed Vitoria's doctrine, a point upon which much argument has been expended in recent years.[2]

The disputants were to direct themselves to the specific issue: is it lawful for the king of Spain to wage war on the Indians before preaching the faith to them in order to subject them to his rule, so that afterwards they may be more easily instructed in the faith?[3] Sepúlveda of course had come to sustain the view that this was "both lawful and expedient" and an indispensable preliminary to preaching the faith, while

Las Casas declared that it was neither expedient nor lawful but "iniquitous, and contrary to our Christian religion".

On the first day Sepúlveda spoke for three hours, giving a résumé of his treatise. On the second day Las Casas appeared, armed with his own monumental *Apologia* which, as he himself stated, he proceeded to read word for word. This verbal onslaught continued for five days until the reading was completed, or until the members of the junta could bear no more, as Sepúlveda suggested. The two opponents did not appear together before the council, but the judges seem to have discussed the issues with them separately as they stated their positions. The judges also carried on discussions among themselves.

It is no wonder that the bewildered judges requested one of their members, Domingo de Soto, an able theologian and jurist, to boil down the arguments and present to them an objective and succinct summary for their more perfect comprehension of the theories involved. This he did in a masterly statement which was then submitted to Sepúlveda, who replied to each of the twelve objections Las Casas had raised. The members thereupon scattered to their homes, taking with them copies of the summary. Before departing, the judges agreed to reconvene on January 20, 1551, for a final vote.

Most of the information available on this second session, which actually took place in Valladolid from about the middle of April to the middle of May, 1551, comes from the pen of Sepúlveda, who discovered, much to his disgust, that Las Casas had availed himself of the vacation period to prepare a rebuttal to Sepúlveda's reply to him. To this last blast Sepúlveda made no rejoinder "because he saw no necessity; indeed, the members of the junta had apparently never read any of the replies", but he appeared again before the junta and expounded his views on the meaning of the bulls of

Alexander VI. It was probably at this time that Sepúlveda composed his paper entitled "Against those who depreciate or contradict the bull and decree of Pope Alexander VI which gives the Catholic kings and their successors authority to conquer the Indies and subject those barbarians, and by this means convert them to the Christian religion and submit them to their empire and jurisdiction." Sepúlveda stated that much of the discussion at this session revolved around the interpretation of the papal bulls of donation, that the Franciscan judge Bernardino de Arévalo strongly supported his case, but that when he wished to appear again the judges declined to discuss the issue further.

Unfortunately whatever records of the proceedings of the Council were kept have been lost, or at least have not yet come to light. The arguments presented by the two opponents are therefore our only present source. Sepúlveda set forth his position from notes, drawing up no formal brief, but following closely the arguments previously developed in his *Demócrates* in dialogue form, which had circulated widely in Spain in the years preceding the disputation. Leopoldo, "a German considerably tainted with Lutheran errors", takes the part of the man who believes the conquest unjust, while Sepúlveda, speaking through Demócrates, kindly but firmly opposes Leopoldo's ideas and convinces him in the end of the complete justice of wars against the Indians and the obligation of the king to wage them.

The fundamental idea put forward by Sepúlveda was a simple one and not original with him. Thomas Aquinas had laid it down, centuries before, that wars may be waged justly when their cause is just and when the authority carrying on the war is legitimate and conducts the war in the right spirit and the correct manner. Sepúlveda, applying this doctrine to the New World, declared it lawful and necessary to wage war against the natives there for four reasons:

1. For the gravity of the sins which the Indians had committed, especially their idolatries and their sins against nature.

2. On account of the rudeness of their natures, which obliged them to serve persons having a more refined nature, such as the Spaniards.

3. In order to spread the faith, which would be more easily accomplished by the prior subjugation of the natives.

4. To protect the weak among the natives themselves.

It is not necessary to reproduce here the multitude of authorities marshalled by the disputants on Sepúlveda's four propositions. Both men devoted most of their time to the point on which the king sought advice: "How can conquests, discoveries, and settlements be made to accord with justice and reason?" The Valladolid dispute, therefore, must be considered the last great controversy held in Spain to determine the regulations for conquistadores and the proper way to preach the faith. We may note that these old problems, raised in 1513 shortly after the Laws of Burgos were promulgated, and responsible for the adoption of the famous Requirement—of which Las Casas once said that he did not know whether to laugh or weep on reading it—were still unresolved in 1550.

The arguments of Las Casas require little detailed examination. He made a few simple points over and over, with numerous examples and references from the copious literature he had studied, and there is no real question on what he actually meant to say.

The judges at Valladolid appear to have shared the view of the Scottish philosopher who declared "Blessed are they that hunger and thirst after justice, but it is easier to hunger and thirst after it than to define precisely what it means". For they enquired of Las Casas exactly how, in his opinion, the conquest ought to proceed. He replied that, when no danger threatened, preachers alone should be sent. In particularly dangerous parts of the Indies, fortresses should be built on the borders and little by little the people would be won over to Christianity by peace, love, and good example. Here it is clear that Las Casas never forgot and never abandoned his plans for peaceful colonization and persuasion. This proposal has much in common with the idea, put forward by the Catalan mystic Ramón Lull two centuries before, that Spain should Christianize the Moslem world peacefully by establishing a chain of missionary groups at strategic points from Andalusia through north Africa to the Bosphorus. It is clear, too, from the way Las Casas and his Dominican brothers had proceeded in their peaceful persuasion work in Guatemala, that the result Las Casas wanted was a tight control of the Indians by ecclesiastics in paternal but supreme command, like the later achievement by the Jesuits in their famous Paraguayan missions. The plan proposed by Las Casas also bears some similarity to the mission system which Spain actually used in later years to Christianize the provinces north of Mexico including California, New Mexico, and Texas.

Las Casas never diverged from the view he had originally stated years before in *The Only Way of Attracting All People to the True Religion*. His complete thought will not be known until the extensive *Apologia* he read in large part to the judges at Valladolid is available, but it is unlikely that any startlingly new information will be found there.

Sepúlveda's real doctrine, on the other hand, has long been in doubt. He himself was never satisfied that he was understood. In recent years there has arisen a vigorous school in both English- and Spanish-speaking lands to explain and defend his position. Some writers have attempted to show that his doctrine has not been well known to the world and was even suppressed because of the influence of Las Casas. The fact is, on the contrary, that the summary made by Domingo de Soto at the request of the junta and printed at

Sevilla in 1552 by Las Casas presents a concise view of the main points at issue, and Sepúlveda's basic thoughts on just war were included both in a contemporary work issued in Rome and in his *Opera* published in the latter part of the eighteenth century.[4] It is true that Sepúlveda's doctrine has been incompletely understood, partly because his treatise underwent many revisions. Fortunately a new edition appeared in 1951, prepared by the painstaking Latinist Ángel Losada, and the student who wishes to know Sepúlveda's doctrine on just war against the American Indians will henceforth depend upon this edition.[5] Although some of Losada's interpretations of Sepúlveda's ideas seem questionable, his text appears to be the definitive edition of this major document. It is better organized and more complete than earlier ones, omits some of the harsher expressions on the nature of the Indians, and corrects what Losada points out as a number of mistranslations in earlier editions. Losada believes that the text he has published represents the true thought of Sepúlveda, and the reader who follows the minute and exhaustive collation of the four manuscripts he provides is bound to agree.

Attention will be centred now, therefore, on trying to analyse Sepúlveda's ideas as presented in the new Losada text. The two great questions treated by Sepúlveda at Valladolid were:

1. What justifies war against the Indians?
2. How should this just war be waged?

Because of their complexity, these two closely related questions will be given separate treatment.

The Great Debate at Valladolid, 1550-1551: The Application of Aristotle's Theory of Natural Slavery to the American Indian

THE most startling argument developed at Valladolid, certainly the most vigorously disputed then and now, was the second justification propounded by Sepúlveda for the Spaniards' overlordship: the "natural rudeness and inferiority" of the Indians which, he declared unequivocally, accorded with the doctrine of the philosophers that some men are born to be natural slaves.[1] Indians in America, he held, being without exception rude persons born with a limited understanding and therefore to be classed as *servi a natura*, ought to serve their superiors and their natural lords the Spaniards. But how can this be? innocently asks Leopoldo of Demócrates. Aren't all men born free, according to the doctrines of the jurists? Have they been joking all the time? No, replies Sepúlveda through the mouth of Demócrates, the jurists refer to another kind of slavery which had its origin in the strength of men, in the law of nations, and at times in civil law. Natural slavery is a different thing.

Philosophers, he explains, use the term natural slaves to denote persons of both inborn rudeness and of inhuman and barbarous customs. Those who suffer from these defects are by their nature slaves. Those who exceed them in prudence and talent, even though physically inferior, are their natural lords. Men rude and backward in understanding are natural slaves and the philosophers teach us, adds Sepúlveda, that prudent and wise men have dominion over them for their welfare as well as for the service given to their superiors. If inferior beings refuse this overlordship, they may be forced to obey by arms and may be warred against as justly as one would hunt down wild beasts.[2]

Spaniards have an obvious right to rule over the barbarians because of their superiority, of which he cites numerous examples. Everywhere Spanish legions have shown bravery —at Milan, Naples, in Tunis, Belgium, France, and more recently in Germany where the heretical Lutherans were defeated. No people in Europe can compare with them in sobriety, frugality, and freedom from gluttony and lasciviousness. As for their true Christian spirit, after the sack of Rome in 1527 the Spaniards who died of the pest, to a man, provided in their wills that the goods they had stolen should be restored to their rightful owners. The meekness and humanitarian sentiments of the Spanish soldiers there, whose first thought after victory was to save as many of the conquered as possible, are well known.[3]

The sack of Rome, as it happens, was a particularly unconvincing example of the benevolence and other virtues which Sepúlveda claimed for the Spanish soldiers, who imprisoned Pope Clement VII and joined the other troops of Charles V in plundering Rome. According to one modern historian, the city was subjected "... to horrors far more awful than those of barbarian days. Lust, drunkenness, greed of spoils and, in some cases, religious fanaticism, combined in truly hellish fashion to produce the worst outburst of savagery in the annals of the period."[4] Even after discounting the inevitable bias of many contemporaries against the powerful Charles V, the testimony of many eyewitnesses remains formidable. Monasteries and churches were burned, nuns violated, pregnant women put to the sword, and no one was safe from the depredations of the unpaid and savage soldiers of many nations who made up the imperial army. Though Spaniards apparently respected holy places and sacred images, "in cruelty and perfidy they even surpassed the Germans", according to one eyewitness account of the revolting actions of the soldiers.[5] Charles V was shocked, and one of his private secretaries, Alfonso de Valdés, hastened to compose a vigorous and eloquent defence of his king entitled *Diálogo de Lactancio y un Arcediano*. Valdés "explained", with many reasons and examples from history, the justice of both the Emperor's political policy towards Pope Clement VII and the sack of Rome. Valdés did not attempt to deny that monstrous cruelties had been committed, but he adopted the attitude that Rome had received a merited punishment.[6]

It is hard to understand today how anyone could have used the sack of Rome to demonstrate the clemency and sobriety of Spanish soldiers without being challenged by someone who knew the facts, and it is even more difficult to comprehend how Sepúlveda in particular could say such things, inasmuch as he had followed the army into Rome and could scarcely have been ignorant of what actually happened, even though he himself had taken refuge in the Castle of San Angelo.[7] However this may be explained, he did in fact cite the sack of Rome as his culminating proof of the superiority of Spaniards over Indians.

He then proceeded to elaborate his version of Indian character. Indians were given over, he wrote, to all kinds of passions and abominations and not a few of them were cannibals.[8] Before the Spaniards arrived they waged war among themselves almost constantly, and with such fury that they considered a victory empty if they were not able to satiate their prodigious hunger with the flesh of their enemies. The Scythians were cannibals too, he recalled, but were fierce fighters, whereas the Indians are so cowardly that they can scarcely suffer the presence of Spanish soldiers, and many times a few Spaniards were able to rout thousands upon thousands of Indians "who fled like women". For example did not the brave and resourceful Cortez, with a handful of Spaniards, subdue Montezuma and his Indian hordes in their own capital? Sepúlveda also condemns the Indians' "incredible sacrifices of human beings, their horrible banquets of human flesh, and their impious worship of idols". And he asks: "How can we doubt that these people, so uncivilized, so barbaric, so contaminated with so many sins and obscenities . . . have been justly conquered by such an excellent, pious, and most just king as was Ferdinand the Catholic and as is now Emperor Charles, and by such a humane nation which is excellent in every kind of virtue?"

These inferior people "require, by their own nature and in their own interests, to be placed under the authority of civilized and virtuous princes or nations, so that they may learn, from the might, wisdom, and law of their conquerors, to practise better morals, worthier customs and a more civilized way of life". The Indians are as inferior, he declares, "as children are to adults, as women are to men. Indians are as different from Spaniards as cruel people are from mild people."

"Compare then those blessings enjoyed by Spaniards of prudence, genius, magnanimity, temperance, humanity, and religion with those of the *homunculi* (little men) in whom you will scarcely find even vestiges of humanity, who not only possess no science but who also lack letters and preserve no monument of their history except certain vague and obscure reminiscences of some things in certain paintings. Neither do they have written laws, but barbaric institutions and customs. They do not even have private property."

Sepúlveda here manifested a strong nationalism, and was in fact the first great nationalistic writer in Spain according to

Rafael Altamira.[9] For, boasted Sepúlveda, did not the deeds of Lucan, Seneca, Isidore, Averroës, and Alfonso the Wise testify to the intelligence, greatness, and bravery of Spaniards, from the time of Numantia to Charles V? "The mere fact that the Indians lived under some form of government by no means proved that they were equal to Spaniards. It simply showed that they were not monkeys and did not entirely lack reason."

It is at this point in Sepúlveda's argument that one is reminded of Gilbert Murray's remark in his *Greek Epic*: "Unnatural affection, child-murder, father-murder, incest, a great deal of hereditary cursing, a double fratricide, and a violation of the sanctity of dead bodies—when one reads such a list of charges against any tribe or nation, either ancient or in modern times, one can hardly help concluding that somebody wanted to annex their land."[10] It is also possible that Sepúlveda, who had spent many years in Italy and was looked upon as somewhat of a foreigner in Spain, was attempting by fulsome praise of his own countrymen to prove up to the hilt his own abounding patriotism.

Sepúlveda having drawn up this dismal judgment of Indian character without ever having visited America, Las Casas did not fail to stress that "God had deprived him of any knowledge of the New World". Although Sepúlveda may have seen an Indian lurking about the royal court, he never mentioned the fact, and had depended on the knowledge of others for his views of Indian capacity and achievement.

The dogmatism of Sepúlveda's utterances is the more striking when one considers the amount of information from many sources then available in Spain. In 1519, when Bishop Quevedo had applied the Aristotelian concept to the Indians, little was known about them, for the conquest had not spread far beyond the islands. It is true that a few European craftsmen such as Albrecht Dürer appreciated the artistic booty despatched by Cortez to his sovereign. Dürer wrote in his diary in 1520, after a visit to Brussels where he saw the gifts presented by Montezuma to Cortez and now publicly exhibited for the admiration of the court: "Also I saw the things which were brought to the King from the New Golden Land: a sun entirely of gold, a whole fathom broad; likewise, a moon, entirely of silver, just as big; likewise, sundry curiosities from their weapons, armour, and missiles; very odd clothing, bedding and all sorts of strange articles for human use, all of which is fairer to see than marvels.

"These things were all so precious that they were valued at a hundred thousand gulden worth. But I have never seen in all my days what so rejoiced my heart, as these things. For I saw among them amazing artistic objects, and I marvelled over the subtle ingenuity of the men in these distant lands. Indeed I cannot say enough about the things that were brought before me."[11]

In 1520 few knew as much or judged as expertly as Dürer the artistic accomplishments of the New World, but by 1550 much of the Aztec, Maya, and Inca culture had come to the notice of Spaniards, and a mass of material had come to rest in the archive of the Council of the Indies. Of course the remarkable mathematical achievements of the Mayas or the art and the engineering feats of the Incas were not fully understood then, but much information was available. Even Cortez, whom Sepúlveda so greatly admired, was very favourably impressed by some of the laws and achievements of the Indians, which greatly surprised the conquistador himself when he considered the fact that they were "barbarians lacking in reason, and in knowledge of God, and in communications with other nations".

So enthusiastic did Cortez wax over Indian virtues that one of Spain's most enlightened and experienced officials in

America, Alonso de Zorita, asked why then Cortez described them as "barbarians". Writing shortly after the Valladolid junta, Zorita enquired: "If these things be true, why call the Indians barbarous people without reason?"[12] He also referred to the widespread idea that the Indians were believed to be human in appearance only, and stated that this "popular error" was even supported in the Spanish edition of the works of St Jerome, though readers could not be sure whether Jerome or his translator was responsible.[13] Many capable and wise persons, Zorita remarked, who had never seen the Indians but who accepted the authority of others who likewise had not seen the Indians, had also fallen into this error.

Zorita himself saw admirable traits in Indian character, pointed out that they were not all alike, and even asserted that Spaniards too would be considered barbarians if some of the standards applied to the Indians were used to judge them. For example, Indians were charged with being childlike because they were willing to exchange valuable gold and silver for silly trifles. But, asked Zorita, were not Spaniards then doing the very same things in their civilized communities? Were they not trading with foreigners daily and getting in exchange unimportant trinkets from abroad?[14] Here Zorita showed a spirit of enquiry completely alien to the attitude of Sepúlveda, who neither knew the Indians nor sought far for information on their customs and abilities.

Few Europeans had ever seen an Indian in the flesh. Columbus and other conquistadores usually brought a few natives to Spain to help dramatize their accomplishments at court. Cortez sent rich presents and two Indians dextrous at juggling sticks with their feet to Pope Clement VII in 1529, perhaps to assist the legitimization process for his four natural sons. As Bernal Díaz describes the scene, when the conquistadores' special ambassador presented the precious stones and gold jewels and the Indian jugglers, "His Holiness greatly appreciated them, and said that he thanked God that such great countries had been discovered in his days".[15]

In 1550 a troop of fifty Brazilian natives was brought to France and performed at Rouen before Catherine of Medici and her court ladies.[16] The Tupinambas solemnly danced and carried on mock warfare on the banks of the Seine, but it was all an exotic ritual which brought the French ladies no more real knowledge of Indians than the acrobats sent by Cortez had given the pope a grasp of Indian character.

More Indians were to be found in Spain than elsewhere, but the total number cannot have been great. Indians loved litigation as much as Spaniards and sometimes even crossed the ocean to present their complaints directly to the Council of the Indies. Las Casas reported to the king in 1544 that he had found a number of Indian slaves in southern Spain,[17] and shortly after the Valladolid dispute he was arguing at court on behalf of an Indian representative from Mexico named Don Francisco Tenamaztle who needed "shoes and a shirt and other things" to dress himself decently.[18] The total number of such Indians must have been relatively small, and on the whole they must have presented a sorry sight to Spaniards. What few glimpses Europeans had of Indians in Europe provided no real basis for understanding them or assessing their cultural power and potentiality.

Even if Spaniards had seen many Indians in Spain and came to know them well, the conquest would still have been a shocking experience to both sides. The Spaniards, for example, made in America their first acquaintance with a matrilineal society. The queens and princesses they met both titillated them and scandalized their sense of propriety. The mores of a society in which the males did not make the rules were different from their own, and, as "civilized" persons have done around the world, they unhesitatingly condemned the unfamiliar culture pattern and proceeded to break it down.[19]

Of course Sepúlveda, like many another European of his day and later, was judging the American Indians by his own standards. As Pál Kelemen has made clear, appreciation of Indian art was long delayed because it differed from European art.[20] And exactly what constitutes the hallmarks of civilization is a matter on which many opinions have been expressed. Cortez, in his *Third Letter*, seemed to consider beggars in the streets as a sign of civilization. He observed that "there were beggars in Mexico as are found in Spain and in other places where there are cultivated people (*gente de razón*)". A foot-soldier of Cortez, the salty and knowledgeable Bernal Díaz de Castillo, in comparing the Indians he had encountered, arrived at the conclusion that the natives of Yucatán had a civilization superior to that of the Cuban Indians because they "covered their private parts", whereas the Cubans did not.[21] The veteran of many a fierce battle against the Indians was scandalized at their religious practices but admired their monuments, the bravery of their warriors, their imposing cities, their impressive ceremonies, and the intelligence of their chieftains.[22]

Sepúlveda also justifies the conquest on the basis of the good accomplished by Spaniards, which, he says, heavily outweighs the bad. In a long and detailed section of the *Demócrates*, he explains that great benefits sometimes involve losses, and here he quotes St Augustine's dictum that it is a greater ill that one single soul should perish without baptism than that innumerable innocent men should be decapitated.[23] At this point he launches into a laudatory account of benefits bestowed by Spain on America.[24] The bringing of iron alone compensates for all the gold and silver taken from America. To the immensely valuable iron may be added other Spanish contributions such as wheat, barley, other cereals and vegetables, horses, mules, asses, oxen, sheep, goats, pigs, and an infinite variety of trees. Any one of these greatly exceeds the usefulness the barbarians derived from gold and silver taken by the Spaniards. All these blessings are in addition to writing, books, culture, excellent laws, and that one supreme benefit which is worth more than all others combined: the Christian religion.

At this point Sepúlveda raised a paean of praise in honour of the kings of Spain for their generosity in making available all the many useful contributions bestowed upon the barbarians, from iron and fruits to wheat and goats.[25] In this he may be following the lead of his hero Cortez who also saw the conquest as a great transfer of culture.[26] How, asks Sepúlveda, can the Indians ever adequately repay the kings of Spain, the noble benefactors to whom they are beholden for so many useful and necessary things wholly unknown in America? Those who try to prevent Spanish expeditions from bringing all these advantages to the Indians are not favouring them, as they like to believe, but are really—in Sepúlveda's view—depriving the Indian of many excellent products and instruments without which they will be greatly retarded in their development.

It may be remarked here that Europeans have often been reluctant to believe that other peoples, particularly "natives", have ever discovered anything. The noted Swedish anthropologist, Erland Nordenskiöld, spent his life proving to reluctant colleagues that the South American Indians were ingenious inventors who discovered and developed all sorts of things—some of them never invented in the Old World.[27] The Italian scholar Antonello Gerbi has demonstrated, too, that many examples are to be found of European disparagement of New World inhabitants and achievements.[28]

Facing Sepúlveda's wholesale denunciation of Indian character, Las Casas composed and presented to the judges

his 550-page Latin *Apologia*, which is his only major writing
not yet published.[29] This juridical treatise, consisting of sixty-
three chapters of close reasoning and copious citations, was
dedicated to demolishing the doctrine Sepúlveda had set
forth in *Demócrates*. Las Casas also seems to have worked out
a summary, designed perhaps for those who might find it
irksome to plough through his detailed argument with its
multitudinous proofs.

In his attempt to disprove Sepúlveda's contention that the
Indians had no real capacity for political life, Las Casas
brought into court his long experience in the New World.[30]
Painting a rosy picture of Indian ability and achievement, he
drew heavily upon his earlier anthropological work, the
Apologetic History, a tremendous accumulation of material on
Indian culture, begun as early as 1527 and completed some
twenty years later in time to hurl against Sepúlveda at the
Valladolid dispute. It was designed to meet the contention
that the Indians were semi-animals whose property and
services could be commandeered by the Spaniards and against
whom war could be justly waged. It filled some 870 folio
pages with many marginal annotations added, which perhaps
explains why it is seldom read.[31] Here he advanced the idea,
which astonished the Spaniards of his day, that the American
Indians compared very favourably with the peoples of ancient
times, were eminently rational beings, and in fact fulfilled
every one of Aristotle's requirements for the good life.

Throughout this welter of fact and fantasy, Las Casas not
only strives to show that the Indians fully meet Aristotle's
conditions, but also develops the idea that the Greeks and
Romans were, in several respects, inferior to the American
Indians. The Indians clearly are more religious, for instance,
because they offer more and better sacrifices to their gods than
did any of the ancient peoples. The Mexican Indians are
superior to the ancient peoples in rearing and educating their

children. Their marriage arrangements are reasonable and conform to natural law and the law of nations. Indian women are devout workers, even labouring with their hands if necessary to comply fully with divine law, a trait which Las Casas feels many Spanish matrons might well adopt. Las Casas is not intimidated by the authority of the ancient world, and he maintains that the temples in Yucatán are not less worthy of admiration than the pyramids, thus anticipating the judgment of twentieth-century archaeologists.

Las Casas at last concludes, from a vast array of evidence, that the Indians are no whit less rational than the Egyptians, Romans, or Greeks, and are not much inferior to Spaniards. Indeed, in some respects, he declares them even superior to Spaniards.

One wonders why Las Casas felt it necessary to construct this truly monumental history on Aristotelian lines and to try to fit into the Philosopher's definition the polity of the American Indians. Was Aristotelian influence so great in learned and court circles of Spain that such a feat was necessary to gain his point? Or did he use Aristotle merely because his opponent had done so and, like any skilful debater, sought to turn the argument to his advantage? Or did he see that the solution of the Indian problem lay, not only in legal protection but above all in establishing the Indians in the eyes of the Spanish community as human beings with a culture which it must respect?[32]

Aristotle indeed enjoyed great authority in sixteenth-century Spain, even though Hernando de Herrera challenged him as early as 1517,[33] and his ideas constituted the "first major current of Renaissance thought".[34] Despite some significant modifications, "Renaissance Aristotelianism continued the medieval scholastic tradition without any visible break".[35] It preserved a firm hold on the university chairs in Spain and the New World, and was even prescribed for the

Indian students who attended the Colegio de Santa Cruz in Mexico.[36] By the second half of the century scholars such as the Jesuit José de Acosta, as a result of experience in America, were laughing at some of Aristotle's ideas, such as those on climate. It greatly amused Acosta and his companions to be in equatorial regions where according to Aristotle it must be blazing hot and to feel cold because of the altitude.[37] In the late eighteenth century, Aristotle was to be condemned by some circles in Spanish America as a "servile sink of errors".[38] But in the sixteenth he reigned almost supreme in Europe and America. Acosta even while exposing Aristotle's error on climate insisted that he would ponder long before questioning any of Aristotle's other ideas. And Las Casas, who had declared before Charles V in 1519 that Aristotle was a gentile burning in hell whose philosophy should be accepted only when it proved consistent with Christian doctrine, was much more respectful towards Aristotle in 1550. At Valladolid he spoke out of years of study as a member of the Dominican Order, which had always emphasized Aristotelian doctrine. He was surrounded by able theologians in the Dominican convent of San Gregorio in Valladolid, and would probably have met opposition among his brothers had he attacked Aristotle directly. At any rate Las Casas denounced Sepúlveda for misunderstanding Aristotle and for failing to admit the diversity among the Indians, rather than the Philosopher himself.

One sympathizes with the struggle required for each contestant to get to the heart of the matter, for Aristotle himself appears to have formed several conceptions of the natural slave, and even such an able sixteenth-century scholar as Hernán Pérez de Oliva found him difficult to understand.[39] In *Nicomachean Ethics* he states that his idea of the slave in no way implies inferiority or inequality due to race or status.[40] In the *Economics* he appears to make a distinction between the slave in theory and the slave in fact.[41] As a recent re-examination of the natural slave concept brings out, however, the slave of the *Politics* cannot know virtue. "He can have no share in happiness or free choice. . . . So long as he remains characterized by his function of bodily service, that function and that alone can give him a share in the common life of man."[42]

The variety of interpretations need not surprise us, for the Aristotelian conception was broad and not set out in exact detail by its author. Aristotle may not have made up his own mind definitely, or the difficulty may originate from the fact that we do not now have a definitive text of what he himself wrote but, apparently, only lecture notes made by a student. In any case, it is clear that every century has interpreted Aristotle anew. Even today the theory has its obscurities, and the literature of explanation and commentary on Aristotle is increasing today at an astronomical rate.[43] One writer states flatly: "Aristotle in no place clearly indicates how a true slave may be known from a free man."[44]

Until recent years, however, it seemed quite certain that the main positions of both Las Casas and Sepúlveda were known. Now two radically new views have been developed which try to place even these matters in doubt. The first view would have us believe that all of Las Casas' thought was "fundamentally Aristotelian".[45] It is true that Las Casas in his argument at Valladolid appears to accept the theory, or at least admit the possibility, that some men are by nature slaves. It is also true that his *Apologética Historia* was put together to prove that the American Indians fulfilled, and in a most convincing way, all the conditions listed by Aristotle as necessary for the good life. But Las Casas never attempts to defend the idea or seeks to extend its scope. Rather, he tries to confine its application to the smallest area possible. He not only denies vigorously that the Indians fall into the category of natural slaves, but his argument tends to lead inevitably to the conclusion that no nation—or people—should be condemned as a whole to such an inferior position. Natural slaves are few in number and must be considered as mistakes of nature, like men born with six toes on their feet or only one eye.

Why then did Las Casas appear to accept Aristotle's theory, even in a limited sense? One possible interpretation is that Las Casas here manifested that realistic and legalistic spirit which characterized a considerable part of his action. Part of his opponent's attack rested upon the allegation that the American Indians were slaves by nature. The defence of Las Casas was not to attack Aristotle frontally but to show that the doctrine was inapplicable to the Indians. At the same time his exposition of what kind of person might fall into this Aristotelian category shows how irrelevant he considered the theory to explain the world at large. One might conclude, therefore, that Las Casas paid lip-service to Aristotle only to refute the application of his doctrine to the Indians. That Las Casas was fundamentally an Aristotelian thinker has yet to be established and this new interpretation of the Valladolid controversy has not gained support.[46]

The second new interpretation concerns Sepúlveda, and requires careful consideration. The most recent writer on the subject propounds the surprising view that Sepúlveda did not mean to apply Aristotle's doctrine of natural slavery at all but intended to recommend a sort of feudal serfdom, and bases the argument on a distinction he finds between two translations of the word *servus*.[47] It must be observed at once that translating *servus* as "serf" rather than as "slave" rests upon conjecture rather than upon what Sepúlveda wrote in his treatise. Sepúlveda had studied Aristotle intensively in Italy under the direction of Pietro Pomponazzi, the eminent Renaissance authority in the field, was painstakingly translating into Latin the *Politics* about the time he was writing his treatise *Demócrates*, and was probably the foremost Aristotelian in Spain.[48] He praised the Philosopher repeatedly,[49] knew many passages of his writings by heart,[50] and specifically recommended to Prince Philip in 1549, while seeking royal support for the publication of *Demócrates*, that he read the *Politics*.[51] At the time of the Valladolid controversy, he was considered one of Spain's foremost scholars and was usually described by his contemporaries as "learned" and "erudite". It thus seems reasonable to suppose that if he had meant the Indians to be classed as medieval serfs and not as Aristotelian "natural slaves" he would have said so unmistakably. Instead, he sets forth, with considerable detail, the proposition that the Indians were born so inferior—so rude, idolatrous, and ignorant—that they may be properly classified as natural slaves in accordance with the theory of the *Politics*.[52] From this proposition flows a practical conclusion. These inferior Indians may be justly warred against and enslaved if they do not recognize that the Spaniards are their natural superiors—again in the Aristotelian sense.

Among the arguments adduced to support the interpretation that Sepúlveda meant serf is a linguistic one: the assertion that *servus* should be translated into Spanish as *siervo* in the sense of serf instead of *esclavo* in the sense of slave.[53] But the standard Latin-Spanish dictionary of Antonio de Nebrija, printed in 1494 and presumably still authoritative in 1550, defined *servus*, the term used by Sepúlveda, as either *siervo* or *esclavo*. The first *Diccionario de la lengua castellana* issued by the Real Academia Española in 1726–1739 also gives *siervo* and *esclavo* as equivalents. And the numerous examples of the way these two words were used in Spanish literature of the sixteenth and seventeenth centuries, as recorded in the imposing word catalogue of the Academia, all reveal that the words *siervo* and *esclavo* were used interchangeably.[54] Thus the translation of *servus* as *esclavo* or slave follows standard authorities, and Sepúlveda's description of Indians indicates that he considers them natural slaves rather than medieval serfs.

Some sixteenth-century scholars attempted to "modernize" Aristotelian doctrine[55] and others made an effort to bring it into consonance with Christian thought by judicious adaptation.[56] Not so Sepúlveda. He had never seen the Indians of America but he knew his Aristotle and applied the natural slavery doctrine literally. The authoritative linguistic usages cited above are not really needed to establish the fact that Sepúlveda meant slave and not serf. His own words must be ignored if any other interpretation is adopted.

The assumption that Sepúlveda meant to recommend serfdom rather than slavery rests also in part upon the fact that he supported the encomienda system, by which the Indians served Spaniards in a serf-like capacity.[57] Towards the end of *Demócrates* he seems to approve encomiendas specifically: he favours the parcelling out of Indians among "honourable, just, and prudent Spaniards, especially those who helped to bring the Indians under Spanish rule, so that they may train their Indians in virtuous and humane customs, and teach them the Christian religion, which may not be preached by force of arms but by precept and example".[58] The important point to be understood here is that he recommends this benevolent arrangement only for those Indians who voluntarily accept Spanish rule and agree to become Christians. We know, from the discussion of Indian character in Book I of *Demócrates*[59] and from his correspondence with Alfonso de Castro—to be described later—that Sepúlveda was convinced that the great mass of Indians would never voluntarily give up their own religion. Force would be required, therefore, for all such people. His approval of the encomienda system and his strong condemnation of the use of force thus apply only to that small number of Indians who would voluntarily accept Christianity and Spanish overlordship. Unless this essential distinction, between the few who voluntarily submitted and the mass who must be warred against as a preliminary to their conversion, is kept clearly in mind, the true import of Sepúlveda's doctrine will be missed.

It must be admitted, though, that the problem is difficult, largely because of Sepúlveda's method of presenting his complex arguments. It is also true that sometimes in medieval Europe the serf had been thought of "in the Aristotelian way as a natural *servus*",[60] and that consequently some confusion existed even in earlier centuries, as St Antonino explained about 1400 in his *Summa Moralis*.[61] But if Sepúlveda meant serf rather than slave he never made his viewpoint clear to any of his contemporaries. Domingo de Soto, the experienced theologian and jurist designated to draw up a summary of the argumentation on both sides, never shows in his résumé that Sepúlveda spoke in this vein, nor do any of his contemporaries who supported or opposed his doctrines. Therefore to establish the authenticity of this twentieth-century gloss—that Sepúlveda did not mean to invoke Aristotle's doctrine of natural slavery—will require proof. Until such evidence has been produced, we must continue to believe that Sepúlveda meant what he said when he applied to American Indians, in meticulous and convincing detail, Aristotle's theory that some men are born slaves, and that they were to remain in this condition as "animate possessions" of the Spaniards, their natural lords and permanent superiors.[62]

The Great Debate at Valladolid, 1550–1551: The Waging of Just War Against the American Indian

THE second problem which Sepúlveda deals with, in *Demócrates*, is how to wage just war against the Indians. Demócrates having convinced Leopoldo that the wars themselves are just, the manner in which they may justly be waged now engages the attention of the two characters.

Sepúlveda clears the way by stating that he understands some wars against the Indians have been made for the purpose of winning booty. These he sternly condemns, and those who wage war with cruelty he characterizes as impious and criminal. But "certain accounts" of the conquest of Mexico which he has recently read, probably the reports by Cortez, show that not all wars in the New World have been motivated by greed or waged cruelly. And of course the fact that some individuals err does not mean that the enterprise as a whole is wrong or the king of Spain unjust. If confided to men who are not only brave but also "just, moderate, and humane", the conquest may easily be carried on without committing any crime and will not only redound to the advantage of the Spaniards but will bring even greater benefits to the Indians.[1]

Now Sepúlveda explains in detail how just war against Indians must be waged. First the barbarians are to be invited to accept the great benefits the conqueror proposes to bestow, to permit themselves to be instructed in the "true religion and the best laws and customs", and to recognize the rule of the king of Spain. If they are thus approached and admonished, "perhaps without using arms", they will submit themselves and their possessions to the Spaniards. If they request an opportunity to deliberate upon the offer, sufficient time to organize a public council and reach a decision shall be granted. If they reject the Spanish proposal, they are to be conquered, their goods confiscated as the property of the conquering prince, and they are to be punished by the usual procedure with the vanquished, that is, by enslavement. If these conditions are fulfilled, the war against the barbarians will be just, even though the individual soldiers or leaders may be moved by greed, and the booty they win need not be restored as would otherwise be the case.[2]

It is curious that Sepúlveda does not refer explicitly to the Requirement or to what happened when Spaniards in past years had actually used this formal legal declaration of war in their operations against Indians. Even more important he seems to have changed his mind on this crucial provision, that barbarians should first be invited or warned to accept the Christian faith and Spanish domination, between his composition of *Demócrates* and his appearance before the Valladolid junta. The correct procedure to wage just war, stressed in his treatise *Demócrates*, appears to be much less insisted upon when he actually argued his case. Even more significant on this vital question is his position after the debate, for in correspondence between the Franciscan Alfonso de Castro and himself, printed for the first time in Appendix A, Sepúlveda goes so far as to ask why any preliminary warning at all need be given such idolatrous people as Indians. Castro, the author of *De Justa Hereticorum Punitione*, supported Sepúlveda's doctrine in general but stated in his book that some kind of exhortation or preliminary warning was necessary. Sepúlveda pointed out in his letter to Castro that no warning had been given in Biblical times nor had Pope Alexander VI mentioned any such warning with respect to the Indians. He believed it very difficult to give and in any case quite useless, as it is clear that "no people will abandon the religion of their ancestors except by force of arms or by miracles". (On an earlier occasion he had made it clear that he expected few miracles in his day.)

Castro seems to have vacillated on Indian questions.[3] Known principally in legal history for his contributions in penology, he held doctrines of some similarity to those of John Major, who had first applied Aristotle's doctrine of natural slavery to the Indians.[4] But he believed that even war against idolaters would be unjust unless preceded by a period of intense and apostolic labours to convert them. One of his opinions, on which Vitoria commented favourably, was that Indians could and should be instructed in all the liberal arts and ordained by the Church.[5] In later correspondence with Sepúlveda, referred to above, he completely reversed his position on the need for exhortations and missionary labours before waging war for he agreed that, if by "prudent conjectures" it could be determined in advance that the idolaters were in fact "pertinacious", they could be warred against justly even without the warning. All this would be in conformity, wrote Castro, with what theologians had said with respect to *correctio fraterna*. He strongly supported giving control over Indians in perpetuity, in a long and detailed opinion written in London and delivered to Philip II there on November 13, 1554.[6]

It is sometimes asserted that these questions of legal and theological justification had no connection with the real world, that the fine-spun theories elaborated in the council chambers and monasteries of Spain had no influence in America. Yet the historical documents available for a study of the conquest prove the contrary. In the very year of the Valladolid controversy, for example, indeed on March 12, 1550, just as Sepúlveda and Las Casas were preparing their arguments, the conquistador Pedro de Valdivia on the far-off fringe of Spanish empire in Chile demonstrated that there was a most practical aspect to the "requirements" and the principles approved by Sepúlveda for handling "pertinacious" Indians. Valdivia announced to his king, Charles V, that on that day he had met and defeated the famous Araucanian Indians in a bloody encounter with a host of their bravest warriors—"the finest and most splendid Indians that have ever been seen in these parts". Valdivia proudly reported that "some 1500 or 2000 were killed and many others lanced". Of the prisoners taken "two hundred had their hands and noses cut off for their contumacy, inasmuch as I had many times sent them messengers and given them commands as ordered by Your Majesty. After this act of justice, when all had been gathered together, I spoke to them, for among them were some *caciques* and leading Indians, and told them that it had been done because I had sent often to summon them and bid them come in peace, telling them to what end Your Majesty had sent me to this land, and they had received the message and not done as I bade them and what seemed best to me for fulfilling Your Majesty's commands and the satisfaction of your royal conscience. And so I sent them away."[7]

We do not know whether this is the kind of "brotherly correction" that Sepúlveda had in mind. Nor do we know how the Araucanian Indians felt about Spanish justice as they went home minus their hands and their noses, though history does record that the Araucanians became exceedingly persistent enemies and were never fully conquered by the Spaniards. As for Sepúlveda, if the attitude he expressed in the correspondence with Castro represents his final thinking on the subject, it would seem that his doctrine permitted undeclared war against all the Indians of the New World, for in Spanish eyes they were all stubborn idolaters. A passage in *Demócrates*, set against this incident of Valdivia's justice, has ironic force: But what greater benefit can they enjoy, asks Sepúlveda, than their submission to the rule of Spaniards whose prudence, wisdom, and religion will bring these barbarians, scarcely men, as far as possible to human and civilized ways by converting them from criminals into virtuous beings, from impious slaves of devils into worshippers of the true God?[8]

Sepúlveda opposes baptism by force, although he holds that the Indians may be forced to listen to the preaching of the Gospel. It was this attempt by Sepúlveda to carry water on both shoulders that led Las Casas to remark that preaching the faith after first subjecting them by force is the same as preaching the faith by force.[9] Sepúlveda's reasoning also reminds the reader today of George Orwell's description of the development of "Double-think" in the future state, in his novel *1984*, when the Ministry of Truth propagates such slogans as "War is Peace", and "Slavery is Freedom". But Sepúlveda felt that despatching missionaries to such people before they are pacified is a difficult, perilous undertaking which produces little or no fruit. The "perverse idolaters" must be not only invited but also compelled to accept what is for their own benefit. No other sure method exists to facilitate the preaching of the faith than to oblige them by force of arms to accept Spanish rule. Even after they had been conquered and while Spanish soldiers were quartered nearby, Sepúlveda points out, Indians killed some Dominicans and Franciscans in Pirito, Chiribiche, and Maracapana. He expresses concern for the lives of missionaries then being sent to Florida without armed protection, all because of a "plan drawn up by certain persons who are much given to working up bold projects which involve toil and danger for others".[10] This is doubtless a jibe at Las Casas who, as we have seen, was extremely active after his return to Spain in 1547 in recruiting friars for America. He was particularly close to the expedition of his old friend Luis Cáncer (specifically referred to by Sepúlveda) who was, in fact, killed shortly after the Valladolid disputation by Indians in Florida.[11]

Sepúlveda recognizes at another point that the time may come when some Indian princes may voluntarily request Christian teaching but he does not elaborate the idea and gives more attention to showing that the papacy strongly supported the Spaniards in their work in America and in their submission of the Indians to Christianity "by the threat or use of force". Sepúlveda is convinced that the Indians will ordinarily receive the new religion only when the preaching of the faith is accompanied by threats such as will inspire terror. Thanks to this felicitous combination, a majority of the barbarians have already been Christianized![12]

Domingo de Soto complained in his résumé of the argument at Valladolid that both disputants discussed subsidiary and marginal matters. In the second book of *Demócrates*, for example, Sepúlveda considers the problem of what should befall the Indians after just war has been waged against them or after they have voluntarily subjected themselves to Spaniards. Even though Losada prints in his recent, and now standard, text of the treatise much new material omitted in other versions, the second book occupies only 38 of the total of 124 pages. Although it does not treat at all the principal issue at stake during the Valladolid disputation—the justice of waging war against the Indians as a preliminary to their Christianization—it provides important information on Sepúlveda's thoughts on minor matters and merits some attention. This shorter portion of the discussion between Leopoldo and Demócrates takes place, we are told, after their vigour has been renewed by a bounteous meal followed by a long siesta.

Today's reader, however, may suspect while reading this section that the disputants' minds had failed to profit much from these refreshments; the arguments wind back and forth in a confused and complicated pattern. Sometimes Sepúlveda appears to contradict a doctrine he approved in Book One. Perhaps this portion of the treatise comes to us revised to meet objections to his ideas raised when they were circulated in manuscript during the years preceding the disputation.

The first question raised by Leopoldo in Book Two concerns the justice of condemning the barbarians to loss of their goods and liberty.[13] Even though they were born to serve their superiors and are idolatrous, must they for these reasons lose their property and liberty? asks Leopoldo. In a long passage, printed for the first time in the Losada edition of the treatise, Sepúlveda makes Demócrates reply that, although barbarians may be true owners of property acquired justly, and some slaves may be very noble and owners of great properties, yet the law of nations and the law of nature provide that to the victor belong the spoils.[14]

The conqueror in a just war may kill his enemy with complete legality or spare his life by enslaving him and confiscating his property. Conquerors, of course, may temper the punishment in the interests of peace and public welfare, and Sepúlveda cites the prudence of some of the ancient Romans who permitted some of their vanquished to go free and live according to their own legislation, others being converted into stipendiaries. Julius Caesar treated the defeated Gauls in a very humane way except for the treacherous Aduatuci, whom he enslaved and deprived of their property. Naturally this clemency will be applied only after the victory is won, and until then Christians will make use of all means necessary to win: "they will kill their enemies and submit them to slavery, despoil them of their weapons and property, and assault and destroy their encampments".[15]

Sepúlveda also makes clear that Indians cannot, because of their sins, under any circumstance wage just war against Spaniards any more than Christians could be justly warred on by Jews, whose "extermination God desired because of their crimes and idolatry".[16] Moreover, ignorance of the law does not excuse the sinner, declares Sepúlveda in a labyrinthian argument wherein he also points out that soldiers must not question whether a war is just or not, as this is not their business. If, following the orders of their ruler in good faith, they fall into error or commit some injury, they may not be held personally responsible.

In the concluding eight pages of *Demócrates*, Sepúlveda establishes a sharp difference between Indians captured in just war and those who surrender to Spaniards because of "prudence or fear".[17] For the first group, slavery and the loss of all their property are their just deserts and it may be presumed that the overwhelming majority of Indians were found in this category. To distinguish the situations of those who surrender peacefully and those who do not, Sepúlveda quotes Biblical authority for putting to the sword all males of cities resisting the Israelites. The American Indians who refuse to submit merit this treatment as well, says Sepúlveda; the Bible refers to "those far-off cities", as well as to the cities of the Holy Land in which those who resist are to be killed to a man.

At this point, Sepúlveda makes one of his abrupt changes and immediately following this bloody counsel seems to say that both Spaniards who conquer and Indians who resist have some justice on their side. If it were not for the Indians' idolatry and their sacrifice of human beings it would be wrong to enslave them or despoil them of their property merely because of their resistance. But their cruelty,

pertinacity, perfidy, and rebellion apparently makes this
necessary, though Sepúlveda recognizes that the pacification
of barbarians will be hastened if they are kindly treated. It
is such interpolations as this which makes Sepúlveda's thinking like a patchwork quilt of many colours and confusing
design. Those Indians who deliver themselves to the mercy
and will of the conquistadores may not be enslaved or
deprived of their goods, Sepúlveda insists, for that would
contravene the law of nations. They may, however, be held
as stipendiaries and made to pay tribute "according to their
nature and conditions".

Even those Indians who voluntarily accept Christianity
and acknowledge the rule of Spain may not, however, enjoy
the same rights as Spaniards, for this would be contrary to
Aristotle's dictum on distributive justice which disapproves
the bestowal of equal rights on persons who are unequal.
Here he launches into an exposition of the various types of
just imperial rule.[18] For those who are "honourable, humane,
and intelligent"—of course he means the Spaniards—a civil
royal authority (*imperio regio*) will be suitable. For barbarians
and those who have little discretion or culture a seigneurial
rule (*dominio heril*) will be more appropriate. This latter type
of dominion has been approved by both philosophers and
eminent theologians for those found in certain regions of the
world who are natural slaves, and for those whose customs
are depraved, or who for other reasons would not otherwise
comply with their duties.

In concluding this exposition on imperial rule, Sepúlveda
gives a somewhat confused picture of how the Spaniards will
actually govern. Apparently there will be both slaves and
free servants, ruled over by their masters with "justice and
affability". The barbarians—and here he must refer to those
who voluntarily accept Spanish rule, not those who are
conquered in just war, since these will be slaves—will be

treated as free persons, "with a certain temperate rule which is both *heril* and paternal, and will be governed according to their condition and the exigencies required by circumstances". In due course, as these Indians become more civilized and better acquainted with Christianity, they will be given greater liberty. Sepúlveda finds in Aristotle a compelling reason to govern wisely the Indians of this category, and quotes him at length to show that empires full of oppressed and resentful underprivileged persons are dangerously unstable.[19] The proper kind of rule will be to control such Indians, "partly by fear and force and partly by benevolent and just treatment", maintaining them in such condition that they will neither be able to revolt nor wish to do so.

Towards the end of the treatise, in a brief passage already referred to,[20] Sepúlveda supports the encomienda system because it will instruct the Indians in civilized ways and the Christian religion.[21] This instruction should be carried on not by violence but by example and persuasion and, above all, without cruelty and avarice. Sepúlveda expressly condemns the intolerable exactions, unjust slavery, and unsupportable labours which some Spaniards have been accused of inflicting on Indians in certain islands. Here he denounces oppression of the Indians almost as eloquently as Las Casas, and concludes his treatise by declaring that the abuses must be remedied so that the loyal Spaniards will not be defrauded of their merited rewards and the conquered people will be justly ruled for the benefit of the conquerors and also for their own sake, "according to their nature and condition".[22] Probably it was a consideration of such passages that has led one scholar to look upon Sepúlveda as a wise statesman advocating a "sane and prudent imperialism",[23] and led another, though he believed Sepúlveda to reveal great weaknesses as a theologian, to describe him as "a good man of

Christian sentiments".[24] What such writers forget is that Sepúlveda, in the main part of his treatise, maintains that the Indians are all natural slaves according to the Aristotelian doctrine, and that their inferior nature justifies a war against them in which all survivors may be enslaved.

The real question debated at Valladolid did not relate to the encomienda system, and those who explain Sepúlveda's failure to win the great debate by asserting that the monarchy could not allow the development in the New World of such a powerful feudal institution as the encomienda, fail to grasp the essential point that the continuance of that system was not then an issue.[25] That burning problem had been resolved when Charles V revoked in 1545 the virtual prohibition of encomiendas that had been decreed in the New Laws of 1542. When Las Casas and Sepúlveda were arguing heatedly before the judges in Valladolid, the real question pending on encomiendas was whether or not they should be granted in perpetuity with civil and criminal jurisdiction. To this question Sepúlveda gives no reply, and does not even refer to the issue. The full story of this perpetuity struggle has yet to be told, and quantities of manuscript material await the investigator.[26] But it has no place here because the question was not really at stake at Valladolid.

Nor was the question of the royal title to the Spanish empire involved in the dispute, even though both Sepúlveda and Las Casas seem to have suggested it was. Charles V was zealous in seeking advice on how best to govern his American dominions, but he did not seriously doubt the justice and legality of his title. Nor did the tribunal at Valladolid care to listen to lengthy disquisitions on the subject; during the second session when Sepúlveda tried to discuss the royal title in the light of the papal bulls, the judges cut him short.[27]

The central issue at Valladolid in 1550 was the justice of waging war against the Indians, and Sepúlveda made plain in his treatise, despite its complex and often confusing argument, that he considered the Indians to be natural slaves according to the Aristotelian concept and the Spaniards amply justified in carrying on war against them as an indispensable preliminary to Christianizing them.

Aftermath of Battle, 1550–1955

(A) *To the Basic Law of 1573*

THE judges at Valladolid, probably exhausted and confused by the sight and sound of this mighty conflict, fell into argument with one another and reached no collective decision. Las Casas stated later that the decision had been favourable to his viewpoint "although unfortunately for the Indians the measures decreed by the Council were not well executed", and Sepúlveda wrote to a friend that the judges "thought it right and lawful that the barbarians of the New World should be brought under the dominion of the Christians, only one theologian dissenting". The dissident was perhaps the Dominican Melchor Cano, who had previously combated the ideas of Sepúlveda in systematic fashion in one of his works, or Domingo de Soto.[1]

The facts now available do not support conclusively the claim to victory of either contestant. The judges went home after the final meeting, and for years afterwards the Council of the Indies struggled to get them to give their opinions in writing. As late as 1557 a note was sent to Cano explaining that all the other judges had rendered their decisions and that his was wanted at once. These written opinions have not yet come to light, except for one: Dr Anaya's statement approved the conquest in order to spread the faith and to stop the Indians' sins against nature, provided that the expeditions be financed by the king and led by the captains "zealous in the

service of the king who would act as a good example to the
Indians, and who would go for the good of the Indians, and
not for gold". The captains were to see that the usual peaceful exhortations and warnings were made before force was
used.[2] Another judge, the jurist Gregorio López, largely supported Las Casas' ideas on the main issue in the notes to his
1555 edition of the *Siete Partidas*.[3]

Immediately after the last meeting, Las Casas and his companion Rodrigo de Andrada made final arrangements with
the San Gregorio monastery in Valladolid to spend the rest
of their lives there. According to the contract drawn up on
July 21, 1551, they were to be accorded three new cells—one
of them presumably for the large collection of books and
manuscripts Las Casas had amassed—a servant, first place in
the choir, freedom to come and go as they pleased, and burial
in the sacristy.[4]

Las Casas did not, however, settle down to a life of quiet
contemplation. The failure of the Valladolid disputation to
produce a resounding and public triumph for his ideas may
have convinced him that his efforts on behalf of the Indians
needed a more permanent record. He was now seventy-eight
years old, weary from half a century of battling on Indian
affairs, and perhaps desirous of using the printing press to get
his propositions and projects before Spaniards whom he
could not otherwise reach. At any rate, he left San Gregorio
and sallied forth the next year, 1552, to Sevilla, where he
spent many months recruiting friars for America and preparing the series of nine remarkable treatises which were
printed there in 1552 and early 1553. It is possible that he had
no intention of publishing these bold tracts for all the world
to see—they included the inflammatory *Very Brief Account of
the Destruction of the Indies* denouncing Spanish cruelty to the
Indians—but only a limited edition for the eye of Prince
Philip and royal councillors. Whatever his intentions, the

treatises were quickly shipped across the Pyrenees where they were promptly issued in numerous English, French, German, Italian, Latin, and Flemish translations. What had been a bitter but private feud in Spanish intellectual and court circles now became widely known in Europe.[5]

The treatises, among them the *Confesionario*, were also quickly shipped to the New World, much to the anger of those Spaniards who held Indians and deeply resented the wholesale attack made by Las Casas on the conquistadores. The tracts served, too, as textbooks and guides to friars scattered over the vast stretches of America, who tried to put into practice the principles set forth therein. The full story of these heroic and little known attempts—some of which are now being revealed through the patient archival work of the Colombian historian Juan Friede—will eventually provide another valuable chapter in the history of the struggle for justice in the conquest of America.[6]

Sepúlveda's part of the treatise which Las Casas printed in Sevilla and which was later translated in England under the title *Here is contained a Dispute or Controversy between Bishop Friar Bartolomé de Las Casas and the Doctor Ginés de Sepúlveda* appears to have given some comfort to the Town Council of Mexico, the richest and most important city in all the Indies; on February 8, 1554, it voted to buy "some jewels and clothing from this land to the value of two hundred pesos" as a grateful recognition of what Sepúlveda had done on their behalf and "to encourage him in the future".[7] It is not known whether these gifts reached him but if they did they would have been most welcome, for Sepúlveda had long been preoccupied with building up his estate. His eulogistic biographer Ángel Losada describes him as "dominated by a desire to increase his property". And, continues Losada, anyone who consults the many documents bearing on Sepúlveda's life in the Archivo de Protocolos in Córdoba

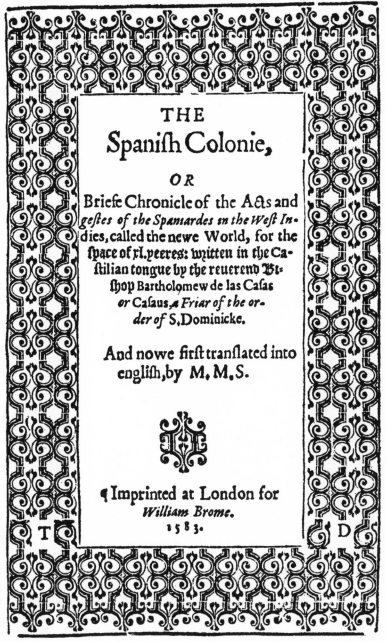

THE
Spanish Colonie,

OR

Briefe Chronicle of the Acts and *gestes of the Spaniardes in the West In-* dies, called the newe World, for the space of xl. yeeres: written in the Ca- ftilian tongue by the reuerend Bi- fhop Bartholomew de las Cafas *or* Cafaus, *a Friar of the or- der of* S. Dominicke.

And nowe firft tranflated into englifh, by M. M. S.

❧ Imprinted at London for
William Brome.
1583.

T   D

FIRST ENGLISH TRANSLATION OF THE LAS CASAS TREATISE *Brévissima relación de la destrucción de las Indias*, WHICH DENOUNCES SPANISH CRUELTY TO THE AMERICAN INDIANS must conclude that he "did nothing in his life except buy, sell, rent, and accumulate ecclesiastical benefices".[8] It is significant that Spaniards in America recognized the importance of the issue sufficiently to want to reward the skill displayed in defending their case. Sepúlveda was so universally considered the outstanding exponent of this point of view that the contemporary historian Francisco López de Gómara did not trouble to justify the conquest at all but recommended that his readers consult "Sepúlveda, the emperor's chronicler, who wrote most elegantly in Latin on this topic, and thus you will be completely satisfied on this matter".[9]

Spaniards were not, however, "completely satisfied" and the battle of words continued. Sepúlveda himself kept the pot boiling by writing, soon after the galaxy of treatises by Las Casas appeared in 1552, a hot blast entitled *Rash, Scandalous and Heretical Propositions which Dr. Sepúlveda Noted in the Book on the Conquest of the Indies which Friar Bartolomé de Las Casas Printed Without a License.*[10]

The positions of both men were by now exceedingly well known in the court and the religious circles of Spain, and according to some writers the Valladolid dispute even echoed in the popular poem "Cortes de la Muerte" of 1557.[11] However that may be, and the evidence is not conclusive, it is certain that the Valladolid disputation provoked the composition during the following years of still more treatises for and against the Indians. The highly respected Bishop of Michoacán, Vasco de Quiroga, noted for his labours on behalf of the Mexican Indians and the application of Thomas More's utopian ideas in Mexico, wrote *De Bellandis Indis* to support the justice of the conquests. According to a letter written in 1553, which Las Casas had in his possession and was found among his papers, Quiroga drew up his statement after he had learned of the stalemate at Valladolid. He had been told that the question was ventilated before "the great concentration of scholars" in such a way as to make it doubtful that agreement would ever be reached on the perplexing matter.[12] Years before he had supported the views of Las Casas on peaceful preaching in his remarkable "Información en derecho sobre algunas provisiones del Real Consejo de Indias", parts of which might almost have been written by Las Casas.[13] Quiroga believed the Indians naturally docile and apt for all arts, and denounced those who found it "inconvenient that they be considered men instead of beasts (*por bestias*)".[14] Some Spaniards hate and abominate the Indians, he said; they accuse them of many evil practices, and are not interested in converting or teaching them. Quiroga testified that he had not seen these charges proved against the Indians and urged that they be neither robbed nor oppressed.[15] Instead he advocated that they should be peacefully converted by Spaniards "going to them as Christ came to us, doing good and not evil to them, pious works and not cruelties, preaching to them, caring for them when they are ill, and doing other deeds of Christian kindness, charity, and piety".[16] Some fifteen years later at Valladolid, in fact at about the time of the Sepúlveda-Las Casas dispute, Quiroga supported the perpetual encomienda for Indians in Mexico.[17] He never supported preaching the faith by force, always had a favourable view of Indian nature, and never invoked the authority of Aristotle to support the idea that Indians were inferior beings. His exact views are not known, however, and our only knowledge of his treatise comes from a refutation of it by Fray Miguel de Arcos.[18] Perhaps further study will place Quiroga's thought in clearer perspective.

Others leaped into the breach too. Sepúlveda declared that one of the judges at Valladolid, the Franciscan Bernardino de Arévalo, not only supported him but also wrote a learned book on the subject, as did another Franciscan, Bartolomé de Albornoz, one of the most noted professors at the University of Mexico when it was first opened in 1553.[19] Albornoz was considered a scholar of "great genius and monstrous memory". He had a low opinion of Las Casas and his doctrine and, while conceding that Las Casas had reached a venerable age and had much first-hand experiences in some parts of the Indies, reminded his readers that Las Casas knew only a part of America. Even his long contact with Indians did not necessarily make Las Casas the supreme authority, pointed out Albornoz, for "some students sit for a long time on benches at the University of Salamanca without learning much". Albornoz saw little value in the many contemporary writings on the encomienda system and the justice of war against the Indians and remarked: "These questions, though very important and discussed by many persons, are perhaps really understood by no one. Those who know how to write lack the necessary experience in America; those who have experience can't write."[20] Albornoz did not support slavery of the Indians and commented ironically that despite the fact that there were about 400 defenders for every Indian, they continued to be enslaved and bought and sold. On one fundamental point he supported Las Casas' idea that it was not enough to save the soul; he asserted, "I do not find in the law of Jesus Christ that the liberty of the soul must be paid for with slavery of the body".[21] The most substantial work, concluded Albornoz whose own manuscript on the subject had been lost at sea, was by the Dalmatian Dominican Vicente Palatino de Curzola.[22] Lázaro Bejarano wrote a treatise against Sepúlveda[23] while Francisco Vargas Mexía supported him,[24] but both documents have disappeared from sight since the sixteenth century. The Dominican theologian Pedro de la Peña strongly opposed both John Major and Sepúlveda in their application of Aristotle to the Indians.[25] One anonymous treatise that has survived, dated 1571, supported the position of Sepúlveda.[26]

In general, opinion was strongly divided on Sepúlveda, as it has been ever since. The Hellenic scholar Juan Pérez de Castro, who achieved a position of eminence among his sixteenth-century colleagues without publishing a single book, was also devoted to Aristotle but doubted that Sepúlveda was mentally well-balanced and stated that "neither in his letters nor in his dialogue can one discover what he is saying because he lacks principle".[27] A number of contemporaries praised Sepúlveda, particularly for his ability to write elegant Latin. On the other hand, Fernando Vázquez de Menchaca, who was probably composing his treatise *Illustrious Controversies* in Valladolid while the justice of wars in the New World was being debated there, opposed Aristotle and those who cited him. In the introduction to this work he struck a blow at those who invoked Aristotle's theory of slavery by asserting that "men try to cover their wars with a cloak of justice", and explained that his purpose was to combat such efforts by studying the most fundamental controversies; thus he might remedy this "corruption of the human spirit, which is almost always caused by the influence and work of those who wish to please powerful and illustrious princes". Vázquez de Menchaca was also certain that, although he had not had an opportunity to study the doctrine of those who believed that Indians might be justly subjugated, the truth was clear to him:

"The doctrine of these authors is an unadulterated tyranny introduced under the appearance of friendship and wise counsel, for the certain extermination and tyranny of the human race. For, in order to practise with greater liberty their tyranny, sacking of cities, and violence, they seek to justify this tyranny with fictitious names, describing it as a doctrine beneficial to those who suffer vexations, whereas in reality never has anything been heard or seen farther from the truth and more worthy of scorn and derision."[28]

About the time Vázquez de Menchaca was writing in Valladolid, the Latinist Francisco Cervantes de Salazar was applying Aristotelian doctrine to the Mexican Indians, but in a far different spirit from that of Sepúlveda. Cervantes de Salazar had served with distinction as a professor at the University of Mexico ever since instruction began in 1553, had been contracted by the Town Council of Mexico to write a treatise against some of the doctrines of Las Casas, and held an extremely low opinion of the Indians.[29] But his dismal view of their achievements and capacity was not as sweeping or as dogmatic as that of Sepúlveda, for he admitted that all nations had some good and some bad elements; some who were leaders, and others who were only able to obey, thus illustrating Aristotle's doctrine. This latter group, very numerous in Mexico, are "naturally slaves (*siervos*) and must be justly warred against, once the necessary procedures have been observed, until they voluntarily listen to and receive the faith".[30] Not even the Town Council of the City of Mexico itself supported the view that Indians had no culture or place in the structure of Spanish government in Mexico. On October 3, 1561, for example, it recommended to the king that six of the twenty-four aldermen (*regidores*) of the city always be Indians in order to make certain that prices be uniform in all parts of the city and to foster the *unión y conformidad* of Indians and Spaniards there.[31]

Unjust wars continued to be fought in America, and were justified by doctrines similar to those of Sepúlveda. Archbishop Gerónimo de Loaysa of Lima called together in 1560 an impressive group of theologians and preachers to draw up instructions for confessors to guide them in determining to what extent encomenderos and others who benefited from unjust wars against Indians should be required to make restitution of wealth acquired by these wars. Severe regulations were approved which made complete restitution necessary in certain cases before the Spaniards might be given absolution. If Spaniards had sincerely believed that war was just because of the idolatry of the Indians, or because they ate human flesh and sacrificed human beings, "or for other similar reasons", they were to be excused from restoring such plunder as they had taken before the arrival of the king's instruction setting forth royal policy. This instruction— evidently putting into legal form the main proposals of Las Casas, especially his ideas on peaceful preaching—seems to be the law he referred to when he asserted[32] that the Council of the Indies adopted his position, and was probably the order sent by the Council of May 13, 1556, to the Viceroy of Peru, Andrés Hurtado de Mendoza.[33]

The junta drew up, and Archbishop Loaysa promulgated, detailed rules—to be enforced thereafter by confessors throughout Peru—on how much conquistadores or their widows and children might be permitted to retain of goods unjustly won. Merchants who sold arms employed in unjust wars were to make reparation unless they were clearly ignorant of the fact that the wars were unjust. These rules came to be standard policy and as such were included in the handbook for missionaries prepared by Alonso de la Peña Montenegro and used throughout America during the seventeenth and eighteenth centuries.[34]

Even Archbishop Loaysa's regulations did not stop the disputes. An altercation took place in the Dominican monastery of Atocha in Madrid in 1561, at which both Las Casas and Philip II were present, during which the Franciscan Juan Salmerón defended the justice of wars against the Indians on account of their "bestial sins and human sacrifices".[35] In Peru, Juan de Matienzo, later famous counsellor of Viceroy Francisco de Toledo, recommended that a junta be held to consider his book *Gobierno del Perú* because of the great disputes on Spanish action in Peru and the deaths of Indians there.[36] The same problems on just war were raised in the Philippines, Chile, and other parts of the empire, and the same contradictory attitudes developed, but this story has been told elsewhere and need not be repeated.[37]

Las Casas, of course, never wavered in his convictions, and in his will, dated March 17, 1564, prophesied darkly: "Surely God will wreak his fury and anger against Spain some day for the unjust wars waged against the American Indians".[38] In the last few months of his life he made a final appeal to Rome for support in his campaign.

The attitude of the papacy to the Valladolid dispute has not yet been analysed, though documents on the subject presumably are available in Rome. After the 1537 bull by Paul III *Sublimis Deus* declaring Indians rational beings, no significant pronouncement appears to have been made by any pontiff, perhaps because Charles V had reacted most unfavourably to this independent papal action, which he considered to contravene his authority in the Indies. Even Las Casas seems to have hesitated a long time before risking royal ire by appealing directly to the pope.[39] Having exhausted all means of support in Spain, or perhaps being so near death that he did not fear to brook even a king's displeasure, Las Casas sent a representative to Pius IV in 1565 with a letter. This "Chantre de Chiapa" had no opportunity to fulfil his mission; the pope died on December 9. The Chantre despatched a letter to Las Casas from Rome on the day Pius V was elected, January 7, 1566, promising to deliver a fresh appeal as soon as Las Casas sent it to him.

The second letter was duly presented to Pius V, who was not only a brother Dominican but a reforming pope as well, determined to exert an important influence in American Church affairs. Las Casas had couched this last important statement of his life in the most energetic terms, urging the excommunication of anyone who declared war against infidels to be just on account of their idolatry or as a means of preaching the faith. Those who believe that infidels are not legitimate owners of their goods or that they are incapable of receiving the faith "no matter how rude or ignorant they may be" should also be anathematized, Las Casas insisted, and informed Pius V that all these matters were proved in a book he was submitting.[40] From the description of its contents, the book was probably the treatise *The Only Way of Attracting All People to the True Faith*, his first treatise, drawn up some forty years before, which had led to the Vera Paz experiment in Guatemala and to the Valladolid dispute. Perhaps death overtook Las Casas before he was able to despatch this treatise proclaiming the efficacy of peaceful persuasion, for it has not yet been found in Roman archives. Pius V must, however, have been influenced by this plea on behalf of the Indians, for he began to draw up bulls and other documents to improve their lot, and even advised the stiff Philip II, who did not relish papal interference, that "the yoke of Christ should be made easy for the Indians".

Renewed papal interest in the Indians did not diminish the Spanish differences of opinion on Indian character, which continued to be aired long after Valladolid. The Dominican Reginaldo de Lizárraga, one of the outstanding religious leaders in Peru during the latter part of the sixteenth century and eventually archbishop of Lima, considered the Indians to have "the vilest and lowest spirit to be found in any people; they seem truly to have been formed to serve others".[41] On the other hand, Pedro de Quiroga at about the same time deplored the attitude of those priests who looked upon the Indians as children to whom Christianity must be taught by cuffs and blows, according to the old Castilian refrain: *La letra con sangre entra*.[42] Indians who failed to attend Mass were sometimes given twenty-four lashes,[43] although in theory, at least, Christianization was still supposed to be, and often was, a peaceful process both in Spanish and Portuguese America.[44]

Even such a devoted and experienced missionary as Bernardino de Sahagún came to have little faith that the New World could be Christianized.[45] This Franciscan, the first European to study Indian culture and language in a serious professional spirit, felt that the Mexican Indians were a sinful people, marvelled at their degradation, and believed in punishment to make them follow the Christian path. He would rouse Indians in the night to beat them, and ingenuously reported how he "lovingly propelled them towards heaven by blows".[46] Yet Sahagún also respected the Indians and their culture, which he studied with such persistence and skill that he is now considered as the father of the study of Náhuatl language and literature.[47]

Despite all differences of opinion and practice, the crown pursued a steady course during the years after Valladolid in the direction of the doctrine set forth by Las Casas—friendly persuasion, and not general warfare—to induce the Indians to listen to the faith. Though Sepúlveda had been allowed to circulate his views widely in manuscript form and had an opportunity to present his ideas in detail at the Valladolid meeting, his treatise *Demócrates*, which originally set off the controversy, was not approved for publication and the standard law of 1573 on new discoveries probably was drawn up in such generous terms because of the battle Las Casas fought at Valladolid. All regulations made for conquistadores after the Requirement of 1513 were superseded by a general ordinance promulgated by Philip II on July 13, 1573, which was designed to regulate all future discoveries and conquests by land or by sea.[48] As Juan Manzano y Manzano has pointed out, the President of the Council of the Indies, Juan de Ovando, knew of Las Casas' doctrines and caused his manuscripts to be brought from Valladolid in 1571 to the court at Madrid for use by the Council.[49] Ovando, one of the most important and least studied crown officials, probably was much influenced by Las Casas' ideas. According to Manzano, Las Casas himself could not have expressed more forcibly the support for peaceful action towards the Indians than was included in the basic law of 1573.[50]

A detailed examination of these provisions indicates how far the king had departed from the early Requirement policy and from the proposals of Sepúlveda at Valladolid.[51] The Spaniards were to explain the obligation resting upon the crown of Spain and the wonderful advantages bestowed upon those natives who had already submitted—a sort of justification by works—so perhaps Sepúlveda's arguments at Valladolid found their echo too in the 1573 ordinances. The Spaniards were charged, furthermore, with emphasizing particularly "that the king has sent ecclesiastics who have taught the Indians the Christian doctrine and faith by which they could be saved. Moreover, the king has established justice in such a way that no one may aggravate another. The king has maintained the peace so that there are no killing or sacrifices, as was the custom in some parts. He has made it possible for the Indians to go safely by all roads and to carry on their civil pursuits peacefully. He has freed them from burdens and servitude; he has made known to them the use of bread, wine, oil, and many other foods, woollen cloth, silk, linen, horses, cows, tools, arms and many other things from Spain; he has instructed them in crafts and trades by which they live excellently. All these advantages will those Indians enjoy who embrace our Holy Faith and render obedience to our king."

It should be remarked, parenthetically, that the crown had long ruled that "all these advantages" must be paid for by the Indians themselves.[52] The tribute exacted of Peruvian

Indians at the time of the Valladolid disputation, for example, was heavy; they were required to deliver money, food, and manufactured goods to their encomenderos who might live forty leagues away.[53]

The 1573 ordinance does not refer to such tribute by Indians or to their obligation to pay for the cost of the benefits being bestowed on them. On the contrary unpleasant topics were avoided, and the law decreed particularly that the word "conquest" should no longer be used but instead the term "pacification".[54] The vices of the Indians were to be dealt with very gently at first "so as not to scandalize them or prejudice them against Christianity". If, after all the explanations, natives still opposed a Spanish settlement and the preaching of Christianity, the Spaniards might use force but were to do "as little harm as possible", a measure that Las Casas never approved. No licence was given to enslave the captives. This general order governed conquests as long as Spain ruled her American colonies, even though some Spaniards could always be found who thought that the Indians should be subjugated by force of arms, because they were not Christians. The disputes leading up to the 1573 law were responsible for a fundamental cleavage among those who wrote on the work of Spain in America. Spanish historiography now became polarized around two extreme and apparently ineradicable points of view. Most historians condemned Spain or exalted her contributions to the Indians, depending upon whether they followed the argumentation of Las Casas or of Sepúlveda.[55]

(B) Since 1573

Neither the discussion at Valladolid in 1550 nor the promulgation of the basic law on discoveries in 1573 put a stop to the debates on Indians. No clear-cut victory for either side was evident after the Council of the Indies promulgated this basic ordinance, which put the ideas of Las Casas and, to a lesser extent, those of Sepúlveda on the law books. Sometimes missionaries changed their minds on the subject of peaceful preaching after actual experience with the Indians. The Jesuit Alonso López had been a stout protector of the natives and disciple of Las Casas until confronted with barbarous Indians on the frontier of Peru. Then López collected a troop of soldiers and led them himself in order to punish the Indians and drive them off. Another Jesuit, Alonso Sánchez, worked hard in the 1580's to promote a "fire and sword" policy against natives in China and the Philippines, but to no avail, despite the numerous and extensive memorials he drew up.[56] He was vigorously opposed by a brother Jesuit, the famous José de Acosta, whose *De Procuranda Indorum Salute* (1588) was the first book on America produced by the powerful order.[57] The first chapter of this treatise, on how to preach the faith to the Indians, is devoted significantly to the topic "Why there is no reason to give up Hope for the Salvation of the Indians."[58] Chapter 2 is devoted to explaining "Why the Salvation of the Indians seems Difficult and Unimportant to Many Persons."[59] Acosta explains that there are not lacking those who believe that the Indians are not sufficiently intelligent to understand the faith,[60] and in another chapter he reproves those who insist on Indian rudeness and incapacity.[61]

He also specifically repudiates the idea that war may ever be waged justly against barbarians because of their crimes against nature, or because of the Aristotelian theory of natural slavery. He describes this doctrine, and then refutes it.[62] At this point he appears to refer to Sepúlveda without mentioning his name, for he remarks that this doctrine was condemned by the universities of Alcalá and Salamanca, as well as by the Council of the Indies which "prescribed very different methods for new expeditions".[63] In these pages Acosta strongly supports the essential doctrines of Las Casas on peaceful preaching, but does not use his name or cite his books. Perhaps this caution on the part of Acosta may be explained by the fact that one of his brother Jesuits, Luis López, was then under accusation by the Inquisition in Peru for holding opinions which were akin to those of Las Casas on Spanish rule in America.[64] Acosta may have found it prudent not to enter directly into the Las Casas-Sepúlveda dispute, but his viewpoint was quite clear. He emphatically believed the Indians capable of understanding the faith and that the way to Christianize them was by peaceful methods. He certainly did not support the encomienda; the only time the earnest Jesuit curses in *De Procuranda Indorum Salute* is in describing the iniquities of this system.[65]

He returns to the subject in his other principal work, the *Natural and Moral History of the Indies* (1590), where he expounds in several chapters the cultural achievements of the Indians.[66] He is not blind to blemishes on their character—he describes graphically their drunken orgies,[67] for example, and at one point calls them a mixture of man and beast[68]—but he praises them greatly and vigorously combats "the false opinion generally held that the Indians are a brutal and bestial people without understanding, or with so little that they scarcely merit the name of men".[69] On the contrary, he asserts that "the Indians have a natural capacity to be taught, more so than many of our own people".[70]

The Franciscan Jerónimo de Mendieta, writing in Mexico at about the same time as Acosta was active in Peru, definitely rejected Sepúlveda's doctrine. He remarked that whatever relevance such ideas may have had in antiquity, the Christian ideal of the equality of all men has superseded them. Mendieta did not accept Las Casas' view on the Indians' capacity but he did defend them, urging that "since the Indians have less intelligence (*talento*) and vigour than we, it is not right that we despise them; on the contrary, we are under more obligation to treat them better".[71] Another Franciscan, Juan de Silva, reproduced in 1621 the ideas of Las Casas, without citing him explicitly, in an eloquent tract.[72] Silva wrote out of a rich experience. He had been a soldier in the epic defence of Malta in 1565, had served in Flanders under the dreaded Duke of Alva, and had been with the Great Armada of 1588 before becoming one of the Friars Minor and working as a missionary for twenty years in Florida and Mexico. He argued, like Las Casas before him, that preaching the faith under the protection of the sword was to adopt the methods of Islam which he wholeheartedly condemned. Nor did he agree with the general view that pioneer missionaries who were sent among savages and cannibals must necessarily have a few soldiers to protect them from being killed and eaten before they had a chance to deliver the Gospel message. "To this I answer," he cried, "let them be killed and welcome, for the Faith was never spread nor preached without the blood of the preachers. And if some are killed, others will be spared; and it is impossible to find a new way of preaching the Gospel to the heathen without shedding the blood of martyrs which is the seed of the Church." In his memorial of 1621 to the Council of the Indies, from which this quotation is taken, he gives several instances of the success of such purely peaceful missions in Spanish America. The same question of peaceful preaching was raised in Venezuela in 1631, and it seems reasonable to suppose that many other illustrations will appear as the manuscripts in American and Spanish archives become better known.[73]

After his death the unpublished writings of Las Casas were kept in San Gregorio monastery, except for brief periods when they were borrowed by the Council of the Indies or by the official historian Antonio de Herrera. Young friars such as Domingo Fernández de Navarrete consulted them; later Fernández showed his familiarity with the Sepúlveda-Las Casas dispute as he carried on his mission work thousands of miles away in China.[74]

During the early years of the seventeenth century Fray Pedro Simón repeated Sepúlveda's arguments in the prologue to his *Noticiales Historiales*,[75] and, later, the historian of the Jeronymite order, Friar José de Sigüenza, concluded that Indians had been born slaves.[76]

The most learned and the most detailed statement made during the seventeenth or eighteenth centuries on the whole complicated question of Spain's right to America and her method of operations there was set forth by Juan de Solórzano Pereira. His *Política Indiana* (1647) was a copious and scholarly defence of Spanish action in America and of the *criollos*, the Spaniards born in America.[77] Solórzano recognized that many supported the opinion of Aristotle that the Indians were "*siervos y esclavos por naturaleza*"; that they could be compelled to obey those who were wiser, and that war against them was justified. But he himself followed Acosta in dividing the Indians into three categories, according to the amount of culture and capacity they had. In his view, only the last group, consisting of naked and ignorant Indians who wandered in forests and mountains, could be included in the category of Aristotle's natural slaves and so treated. But even those Indians who might be warred against so that their idolatry and other vicious habits would be rooted out, must first be properly and repeatedly admonished to stop their evil practices.[78]

During the latter part of the eighteenth century, there were two constant literary campaigns in Europe, one to exalt the Indians as "noble savages", and the other to depreciate the qualities of all inhabitants of the New World. As an example of the one, Cornelius de Pauw held that Americans, both male and female, were physical weaklings and he stated that in some countries the men had milk in their breasts.[79] As an example of the other, exiled Jesuits in Italy thought and wrote extensively about the lands they had left, and developed a considerable literature defending America and Americans. Las Casas and his ideas were well known to these writers. The proposals Las Casas had made in the sixteenth century on behalf of Indian education were remembered in America too; the archives in Mexico contain a petition, signed by several Indian leaders, which "recalled Las Casas with veneration and requested the re-establishment of the Colegio de Tlatelolco to instruct their youth in sacred letters".[80] It was Tlatelolco to which Robert Ricard referred, in his work on the religious conquest of Mexico, when he stated that if the Colegio had not been abandoned by the Spaniards in the sixteenth century and if it had produced at least one Indian bishop for the Church the whole history of Mexico would have been vastly changed.[81]

As the period of independence drew near, the Abbé Gregoire in France attacked Sepúlveda's doctrine, as did the Mexican priest Mier,[82] but to counterbalance these there appeared a Mexican supporter of Sepúlveda who enquired why the system he advocated for the Indians should not be called "*justo y honesto*".[83] In Chile Manuel de Salas protested vehemently in 1801 against the thesis of Sepúlveda and De Pauw that Americans were inferior, and developed as a counter argument the idea that a young and fresh new world no longer needed old worn-out Europe.[84] At the Cortes of Cádiz in 1812, during the discussion whether Indians should be represented or not, Agustín de Argüelles recalled old opinions that they were natural slaves according to the Aristotelian theory.[85] The Mexican scholar José Mariano Beristain de Souza inserted in his standard bibliography in 1816 a long article on Las Casas in which he characterized the doctrine of Sepúlveda as "worthy only of vandals and tigers".[86] Attacks on Sepúlveda were also printed in Peru and Argentina during these turbulent years when Spain was losing most of her American possessions.

The most influential attack on Sepúlveda's ideas in recent years came from the pen of the outstanding Spanish scholar Marcelino Menéndez y Pelayo, who, although he felt that Sepúlveda's treatise was worthy of full publication at the time of the four-hundredth anniversary of the discovery of America, also stated: "Sepúlveda, a classical scholar described in Italy as a Hellenist or Alexandrine, treated the [Indian] problem with all the crudity of pure Aristotelianism as expounded in the *Politics*, showing himself, with more or less theoretical circumlocution, as a supporter of the theory of natural slavery. His thought in this respect does not differ much from that of those modern empirical and positivistic sociologists who believe the extermination of inferior races an inevitable result of the struggle for existence."[87] In the same commemorative year, 1892, when Spain began to study seriously her work in America, Antonio María Fabié staunchly supported Las Casas against Sepúlveda, pointing out that many other sixteenth-century Spanish theologians also supported the basic principles set forth by Las Casas at Valladolid.[88] Today it is still necessary to restate the elementary fact that Las Casas created no new ideas and was not a wild-eyed thinker out of step with his time.[89] One need not go to the other extreme, however, as do some present-day opponents of Las Casas, of dismissing him as merely one among many Spaniards who defended the Indians.[90]

The controversy over the Valladolid discussion becomes sharper and more subtle in the twentieth century. Two of the more radical interpretations have been discussed above. Sepúlveda has also come to be looked upon in some circles as a misunderstood and somewhat abused thinker, especially by those who are not particularly sympathetic to Las Casas. Thus Sepúlveda is described as "a humanist, a noble spirit" who manifests a "virile and sincere attitude", his harsh views on Indian character are referred to mildly as "unwise generalizations", his position on Indian slavery is considered "the balanced sanity of a great mind", or he is simply labelled as a "conservative theologian".[91] Others will have none of this, and damn Sepúlveda as a professional apologist who sold his pen to those who could pay well. One Guatemalan writer goes so far as to couple his name with that of Hitler as a proponent of repugnant racial doctrines.[92]

To at least one student, the Valladolid dispute has been greatly overemphasized; Sepúlveda, to his mind, was "a great humanist and Latinist, but about two centuries behind the times so far as his legal and theological knowledge was concerned".[93] Ramón Menéndez Pidal, usually considered the greatest living scholar in Spain, turned off the whole complicated controversy at Valladolid with a smooth phrase: "The struggle was merely between the humanitarianism of Las Casas and the humanism of Sepúlveda".[94] In every century since the great debate, the dispute has been re-studied and re-ventilated with no loss of conviction or passion on either side. The struggle between the sixteenth-century protagonists has thus itself become a controversy, as defenders of Las Casas or Sepúlveda have sprung up in various parts of the world.

The problem discussed at Valladolid over four centuries ago concerning the proper relations between peoples of different cultures, religions, customs, and technical knowledge, has today a contemporary and sonorous ring. Sepúlveda and Las Casas still represent two basic and contradictory responses to the question posed by the existence of people in the world who are different from ourselves.

VIII

"All the Peoples of the World are Men"

WHY did no clear-cut, public decision follow the noisy dispute at Valladolid on the application of Aristotle's doctrines to the American Indians? We do not know. Was Charles V perhaps too occupied with foreign wars, as a recent writer has suggested, to permit him to spend time on such questions?[1] A more likely explanation may be that the crown wished to achieve a compromise. It could not accept the views of Las Casas without provoking a revolution in America, even though the regulations governing conquests had become steadily milder and more pro-Indian in tone since the harsh and theological Requirement had first been drawn up in 1513. So far had the crown and Council of the Indies gone by 1550 in promulgating laws to protect the Indians that a change of the sort advocated by Sepúlveda, the deliberate use of war as a regular preliminary to the conversion of the Indians, would have been an unthinkable revolution in royal policy. For this reason his treatise *Demócrates* was not approved for printing and his views did not prevail when laws were issued after 1550 to govern the actions and procedures of conquistadores, as they continued their onward rush through the vast lands of the New World and across the Pacific to the Philippine Islands and on to China. The basic regulation of 1573, described earlier, strictly prescribed a peaceful and sympathetic approach by Spaniards, and not a blood and thunder attitude backed up by Old Testament and Aristotelian authority.[2] But the detailed explanation of the benefits conferred on Indians by Spanish rule also showed that the spirit of Sepúlveda partially triumphed; in the listing of the spiritual, economic, and cultural contributions brought by Spain we see revealed all the essential arguments on the work of Spain in America which have ricocheted and reverberated down the centuries.

One may ask why a sixteenth-century dispute which was never formally resolved remains exciting and controversial more than four centuries after it took place. The point to remember is that it dealt with the emotionally charged problem of the meeting of unlike races and that one of these, the Spaniards, brought to the encounter both their strong preoccupation with justice and their military and religious ardour that had impelled them into the long wars now successfully concluded against the Moors. We can never know how the two opposing views of the Indians appeared to the fourteen judges. We cannot even be sure that they recognized that, in effect, one of the most solemn and basic questions ever posed to a civilization had been laid before them: what was the nature of the folk inhabiting the lands being overrun by the dynamic culture of Spain, and how were they to be dealt with? These were the urgent and inescapable questions, underlying the immediate practical problems relating to wars of conquest and Christianization, which baffled Spain's learned men in 1550–1551.

Exasperation with the human personalities of one or the other of the controversial protagonists, and indignation or boredom over their exaggerations also probably played a part in the indecisions of the judges at Valladolid. Even Domingo de Soto, who in general supported his brother Dominican's position and who was so highly respected a member of the junta that he was designated by the group to draw up an absolutely neutral résumé of both arguments for the judges to use in reaching their decision, found himself entering into the fray. At one point Soto wrote down, and Las Casas printed the statement verbatim as a part of the summary in 1552, that Las Casas said "more than was necessary in reply to Dr Sepúlveda", and on another matter Soto could not refrain from observing that Las Casas was wrong.[3] Few of the scholars subsequently drawn into the discussion have escaped strong reactions to one or the other of the debaters, or to both. Spanish patriotism, which sought and still seeks to destroy the "black legend" of Spanish cruelty, and Spanish idealism, which is enamoured of the "golden legend" of Spanish wisdom, accomplishments, and sense of responsibility in the New World, also account for much of the emotion generated by the great debate.

The problems with which Las Casas and Sepúlveda wrestled were of course not new and, in fact, were older than Aristotle. As the classicist Tarn has written, in Greek times all non-Greeks were ordinarily called barbarians and often regarded as inferior people, though occasionally Herodotus or Xenophon would suggest that certain barbarians possessed some qualities which deserved consideration, such as the wisdom of the Egyptians or the courage of the Persians. Aristotle's model state was a small aristocracy of Greek citizens ruling over a barbarian peasantry who cultivated the land for their masters and had no share in the state. He also held a very flattering view of Greek character.[4] Alexander did not follow the precepts of his teacher Aristotle but divided men into good and bad without regard to their race. "For Alexander believed that he had a mission from the deity to harmonize men generally and be reconciler of the world, mixing men's lives and customs as in a loving cup . . . to bring about, as between mankind generally, *Homoneia* and peace and fellowship and make them all one people. . . . Plutarch makes him say that God is the common father of all mankind."[5]

After Valladolid, and indeed until today, the problem of the basic nature of other peoples different from ourselves in colour, race, religion, or customs has given rise to the most diverse and often inflammatory opinions. It might be said that the idea of the unfitness of natives and their inferiority to Europeans appeared in whatever far corners of the world Europeans reached. Protestants as well as Catholics found themselves embroiled in these questions and afflicted with the same doubts. The French missionaries sent by Calvin to Brazil a few years after Sepúlveda's 1550 attack on Indians found the natives difficult to work with and came to doubt whether they could ever become true members of their faith.[6]

Englishmen, too, adopted what might be called the standard cliché on Indian nature; William Cuningham, in one of the earliest descriptions of Indians to appear in England, had this to say in 1559: "The people bothe men and women are naked, neither suffer they any heare to growe on their bodies, no not on their browes, the head excepte. . . . There is no law or order observed of wedlocke, for it is lawful to have so many women as they affect, and to put them away with out any daunger. They be filthy at meate, and in all secrete acts of nature, comparable to brute beastes."[7] Occasionally a defender of the Indians arose in the English colonies, such as Captain George Thorp of Virginia, but his advocacy of education and fair dealing for the natives did not win much support, and he himself was killed in the 1622 massacre.[8] A few of the Puritan clergy in America asserted that the Indians were children of the devil who might profitably be wiped out and their lands appropriated.[9]

When the English colonists met natives their reaction was not very different from that of Sepúlveda and his supporters. The Indian views of one New England assembly are expressed with perfect simplicity in the sequence of resolutions it is said to have adopted in the 1640's:

"1. The earth is the Lord's and the fullness thereof. Voted.

"2. The Lord may give the earth or any part of it to his chosen people. Voted.

"3. We are his chosen people. Voted."10

Southern colonists during the eighteenth century despised the natives they encountered. John Lawson declared in 1714, referring to the Carolina Indians: "We look upon them with Scorn and Disdain and think them little better than Beasts in Human Shape."11 The prominent Quaker John Archdale included in his report on the disappearance of Indians in the Carolinas the statement that Providence had reserved the extermination of the Indians for the "*Spanish* Nation, and not for the *English*, who in their Natures are not so cruel". Moreover, "the Hand of God was eminently seen in thining the *Indians*, to make room for the English . . . it at other times pleased Almighty God to send unusual Sicknesses amongst them, as the Smallpox, to lessen their Numbers; so that the *English*, in Comparison to the *Spaniard*, have but little *Indian* Blood to answer for". Archdale did not wholly excuse the English in their treatment of the Indians, but he did conclude that for the killing of Indians "it pleases God to send . . . an Assyrian Angel to do it himself" and pointed out a final "Example of God's more immediate Hand, in making a Consumption upon some *Indian* nations in *North Carolina*".12

The nineteenth century witnessed a luxurious growth of disparaging attitudes towards natives, as European expansion brought about a great increase in contacts between peoples of widely varying culture patterns. In the first half of the century, frequent efforts were made in British parliamentary debates on the abolition of the Negro slave trade to prove that the American Negro had degenerated from a higher culture or was incapable of improvement. And "missionaries, seeking to explain small returns on investments made by homeland congregations in the foreign field, discoursed on the tendency of degraded people to relapse, after conversion, to a prior state of paganism".[13]

Echoes of the problems and attitudes of sixteenth-century Spaniards were also heard in the islands of the Pacific. The early missionaries to Hawaii wondered whether the natives there were men or "a link in creation connecting men with brutes".[14] When the Queensland "blackbirders", or kidnappers, were recruiting a labour supply by force in the Pacific "great stress was laid on the civilizing and humanizing influences of regular employment in the Christian land of Queensland. It was pointed out that the head-hunting cannibal savages of the New Hebrides and of the Solomons might be expected, under these uplifting influences, to turn into model citizens, pious, painstaking, and humane.[15] When "Dr Wardell of Sydney defended an Englishman charged with the murder of a Black, he argued from Lord Bacon, Puffendorf, and Barbeyrac, that savages who fed upon human flesh (as the Australians were by him assured to do), were proscribed by the law of nature; consequently it was no offence to slay them".[16]

Scientific circles also were agitated by these questions. Dr Hunt, founder of the Anthropological Society of London, strongly opposed the doctrine of human equality and thought that it would be as difficult for an aboriginal Australian to accept civilization as "for a monkey to understand a problem of Euclid".[17] The Anthropological Society of Paris listened in 1856 to disputes on the relative perfectibility of white and coloured races. Gratiolet delivered himself there of the conviction that "the cranium (of the Negro) closes itself upon the brain like a prison. It is no longer a temple divine . . . but a sort of helmet for resisting heavy blows".[18] This kind of discussion went on among the French savants for twenty years.

Yet the facts of Indian achievements, when known, made

some men wonder whether white Europeans were the only civilized people in the world. Even in these years, before archaeologists had studied intensively the ruins of Maya temples, John L. Stephens asked himself this question while contemplating Copán: "Who were the people that built this city? . . . America, say historians, was peopled by savages; but savages never reared these structures, savages never carved these stones. . . . Architecture, sculpture, and painting, all the arts which embellish life, had flourished in this overgrown forest; orators, warriors, and statesmen, beauty, ambition, and glory had lived and passed away, and none knew that such things had been, or could tell of their past existence."[19]

A school of anthropologists developed in the United States before the Civil War which was committed to showing that the Negro "was no real human being, but a domestic animal". One of the prominent members of this group, which cited Aristotle's natural slavery ideas as justification, was Glidden, who held that "there is no such thing as a common human nature. . . . White men and red men, yellow men and black men, have no more original relationship to each other than the bears of the pole to the tigers of Africa. . . . The blacks do not belong to the same creation as the whites. . . . Their organization dooms them to slavery, and precludes them from improvement."[20] Gabriel René-Moreno, the outstanding nineteenth-century Bolivian historian and bibliographer, held that Christianity was for white people alone. He believed that inferior beings, such as Indians, could not understand Christianity nor could it be adapted to their needs. He was a fervent disciple of Darwin and Spencer, and held that the superior whites would eventually absorb or supplant the Indians.[21]

Such ideas are by no means dead today and affect, among other things, the writing of history. The late Ulrich B. Phillips, the historian of Negro slavery in the United States who "unquestionably made the largest single contribution to our present understanding of southern slavery", began with the basic assumption that the Negro was inherently inferior though he did not quote Aristotle in justification.[22] Jawaharlal Nehru has set down in his *Autobiography* the effect on Indian thought of British versions of their history. "History and economics and other subjects that were taught in the schools and colleges were written entirely from the British imperial viewpoint, and laid stress on our numerous failings in the past and present, and on the virtues and high destinies of the British."[23] So far as the history of Spanish America is concerned, the attitude of the historian—whatever his nationality—towards the Indian and his culture has always been and still is a principal and sometimes determining ingredient in his work.

Many other views on this subject could be given, for the literature is vast, but enough has been noted to suggest the general lines of opinion. It needs to be stressed, though, that the present resistance to desegregation in the United States, and the theory and practice of *Apartheid* in South Africa demonstrate that even today some whites would condemn a whole race to permanent inferiority.[24] If any American yields to the sin of complacency while contemplating the 1550 struggle in Spain, let him read the documented description of the travail of Negroes in the United States during the last quarter of the nineteenth century compiled by Rayford W. Logan, *The Negro in American Life and Thought. The Nadir 1877–1901*.[25] And if anyone attempts to dismiss this monograph as of merely historical value, let him consult the work by S. G. and M. W. Cole, *Minorities and the American Promise: The Conflict of Principle and Practice*.[26] Or let him read the daily newspaper.

What the natives of other continents have thought of Europeans is a story for which relatively little information is available. What is known indicates that the natives also held derogatory ideas about Europeans. The several Bantu tribal groups in South Africa, for example, regarded the whites as less than human and at first did not even refer to them as "people" (*abantu*). Special names had to be coined. The Zulus called whites "those whose ears reflect the sunlight" and the Sothos knew them as "those having the colour of a yellowish claypot".[27] Like some sixteenth-century Spaniards and seventeenth-century Puritans, the Bantus feel themselves to be the elect of all humanity, though this racial pride exhibits itself differently in each tribal group. The Zulus call all other tribes "animals" and themselves "The People". Sothos use derogatory terms to convey the idea that persons not born into their tribe are less than human and may therefore be despised.[28] From these examples we see that both Aristotle and Sepúlveda have something in common with the natives of Africa! Probably future historians of European imperialism will give more attention to the attitudes of native peoples; Lowell J. Ragatz has found that gross distortion mars the present literature on the subject. He believes that one of the important causes of this distortion is the "pucka sahib" complex—the "naïve assumption by western writers that occidental ways are superior to all others and that Christianity, the dominant faith of the West, is the True Revelation".[29]

What importance may be attached to the Valladolid dispute, the first full-length discussion in modern times of relations between peoples of different cultures? Was this conflict, despite all the learned citations of divine and natural law, merely an example of what Reinhold Niebuhr had in mind when he wrote that "most rational and social justifications of unequal privilege are clearly afterthoughts. The facts are created by the disproportion of power which exists in a given social system. The justifications are usually dictated by the men of power to hide the nakedness of their greed, and by the inclination of society itself to veil the brutal facts of human life from itself."[30] Juan Friede expresses somewhat the same thought when he states that the two diametrically opposed groups in Spain—the "colonialists" and the "indigenists"—represented essentially divergent economic and political interests, in spite of all their references to St Thomas, St Augustine, and Aristotle.[31] A modern satirist such as George Orwell, whose bitter view of the future as set forth in his novel *1984* has already been referred to, would probably see in the 1573 law, which abolished the word "conquest" and substituted "pacification" to describe Spanish action in America, a splendid opportunity for his Ministry of Truth to coin another slogan, "Conquest is Pacification".[32]

Preaching and practice were sometimes different. The efforts of Domingo de Santo Tomás and other Dominicans in Peru who sought to win recognition for Indian cultural achievements did not bear fruit in their own order, for "the Dominicans do not seem to have received any Indians or those with Indian blood into their ranks".[33] A chasm yawned between the Spaniards and the Indians throughout the colonial period, and the Liberator San Martín found it necessary to issue his famous order in the revolutionary days of the early nineteenth century. "Henceforward the indigenous inhabitants of Peru shall not be called Indians, but Peruvians."[34] But the Revolution and the early Republican period witnessed no significant improvement in the position of the Indian, and the philosopher Alejandro O. Deustúa (1849–1945), who was influential in the formulation of educational policy in Peru, stated pessimistically: "The Indian is a machine and cannot be anything else."[35] Indians were, he believed, biologically incapable of development.

The gulf continues to yawn today; a contemporary writer declares that aristocratic society in Lima, Peru, is "as far distant from the native population as a New York banker is from a Mexican Indian".[36] Always, too, fundamental problems and basic attitudes are linked; when a European educator once asked the Mexican José Vasconcelos: "And how are you going to resolve the Indian question? Have you already considered the techniques which you are going to use to educate them?" Vasconcelos replied: "No—we are simply going to treat them like human beings, with Christian principles."[37]

In the end, no simplification of the controversy at Valladolid in 1550 is completely satisfactory. Though the application of Aristotelian ideas to the Indians seems a fairly clear-cut issue, the questions discussed there remain complicated; not only have different conclusions been reached by men through the centuries, but individuals change their minds on the subject. Enrique de Gandía, for example, who sadly confesses at the beginning of his volume on *Francisco de Vitoria y el nuevo mundo* that "all the philosophical doctrines and evangelical methods produced exceedingly bad results", changes his mind later on.[38]

We may conclude, however, that ideas were involved in the conquest and deeply involved. Perhaps the clash of Las Casas and Sepúlveda at Valladolid is, above all, the most dramatic incident in the long series of events that make up the story of the Spanish struggle for justice in the conquest of America. It is a complex struggle, in which learned and dedicated men of the same nation were ranged against one another bitterly and irreconcilably divided. Besides ideas, the urge for economic advantage, the clash of personalities, and the over-riding interest of the crown all played their part in the decisions reached and measures undertaken. At times the dedication of men like Las Casas to the proposition that the conquest must proceed peacefully was decisive. The Indians might have been treated like the other non-Christians known to Spaniards; it is significant that the questions on the treatment of Indians arose shortly after the Jews were expelled from Spain. To the historian familiar with the Spanish determination to assimilate or expel these people in the late fifteenth-century drive for ethico-religious unity in Spain, Spain's attitude towards the American Indian will seem remarkably mild. True, the Indian had not known Christianity—although a few Spaniards believed that the Apostle Thomas had evangelized America centuries before and that the Indians were apostates who had fallen away from the faith. But sounder views prevailed and the Indians were never considered fit subjects for the attention of the Inquisition. It was indeed fortunate for the Indians that Las Casas, along with Francisco de Vitoria and Domingo de Soto, emphasized the great distinction between wars against the Indians and those against the Moors and Turks.[39] The brutal doctrines of ecclesiastics and the even more brutal practices of other Spaniards towards the Moors and Jews at the end of the fifteenth century, when the conquest of America was just beginning, show what might have occurred in the New World.[40] The same may be said of the Portuguese as well; Jews were sometimes dragged by the hair to the baptismal font in medieval Portugal.[41]

Today it is becoming increasingly recognized that no other nation made so continuous or so passionate an attempt to discover what was the just treatment for the native peoples under its jurisdiction than Spaniards, not even the Portuguese. Though more akin to the Spaniards than were other sixteenth-century colonizers, they suffered fewer scruples concerning the treatment of native people in the development of their vast and varied empire. Pedro Alvares Cabral, discoverer of Brazil in 1500, carried with him detailed instructions which provided that the ecclesiastics were to explain the faith to the Moors and idolaters they found with "*amoestações e requerimentos*" urging them to abandon their "*idolatrias, diabólicos ritos e costumes*". If they refused to accept the faith or to permit peaceful commerce, the Portuguese were to wage "*crua guerra*" against them.⁴² The Portuguese did attempt in 1561 to legalize war against the Emperor of Monomotapa by the discussion of the problem by a group of theologians designated *Mesa de Conciencia*, but this was an isolated instance of concern with the problem of just war against natives, as is clear from the scanty sixteenth-century Portuguese literature on the subject.⁴³ Brazilian Indians were called "beasts" and some Portuguese maintained that therefore it was lawful to enslave them, but no full-scale controversy arose as in Spanish America and no Portuguese writer invoked Aristotle to justify slavery.

Some incidents of interest in Portuguese-speaking lands may be noted. The Jesuit Leonard Nunes, preaching to the planters of Brazil at Bahia in 1549, declared: "No Christian can save his soul, if he detains the vital goods of other men. By the law of Nature the lives of these Indians are their own. By what just title have you appropriated them to yourselves? You say that this is none of my business. I tell you that it is so much my business that I and my fellow priests are ready to lay down our lives for this just cause."⁴⁴ Even more significant were the efforts of another Jesuit, Antonio Vieira, in the seventeenth century to protect the natives of Brazil. His life and achievements have not yet received their full due, at least in the English-speaking world.⁴⁵ But the historian João de Barros probably represented Portuguese attitudes fairly accurately when he wrote, at about the time of the Valladolid dispute, that the Church gave Portuguese a free hand to make war without provocation on non-Christian peoples, to reduce them into slavery and to seize their lands, since they were "unjust possessors of them".⁴⁶ The infidel, in the eyes of the Portuguese, had neither rights of property nor personal rights. The salvation of his soul justified the loss of his personal liberty.

The doctrine supported by Las Casas and the majority of the numerous Spaniards who wrote or spoke on the subject was never so easily arrived at. It is this Spanish concern for the welfare of the Indians that has appealed particularly to Spanish Americans[47]; in Cuba Enrique Gay Calbó has gone so far as to declare: "We, the American descendants of Spaniards . . . believe that the true Spain is not that of Sepúlveda and Charles V but that of Las Casas and Vitoria."[48] Some Spaniards have also come to see that the general ordinance of 1573 to regulate all future conquests, and the many other laws on behalf of the Indians, would never have been promulgated if Sepúlveda's ideas on just war against the Indians had triumphed at Valladolid.[49] If violence and intolerance are among the characteristics of the Spanish people as one of their greatest historians, Rafael Altamira, declared,[50] the struggle within themselves to permit the triumph of mildness and Christian persuasion, even though the victory was never complete, becomes the more remarkable. Yet this spirit was so firmly entrenched in the minds of those who devised the law that Chinese converts in the Philippine Islands were excused from cutting off their pigtails as a visible sign of their entrance into the new faith. After a sharp controversy on the subject in Manila, the crown itself took notice of this baptismal problem—just as Charles V had done half a century before when Las Casas insisted on proper instruction of the Indians—and decreed by royal instruction of July 13, 1587, that the Chinese need not cut their hair, since this greatly distressed them and might even occasion their deaths if they returned to mainland China. Instead, the bishop of Manila and his missionaries were instructed to treat them "with prudence and intelligence, and with the kindness and mildness required to nurture such new and tender plants".[51]

This spirit was also made an integral and permanent part of the Laws of the Indies when it was declared in that great code, printed in 1680: "War cannot and shall not be made on the Indians of any province to the end that they may receive the Holy Catholic Faith or yield obedience to us, or for any other reason."[52] Official recognition that the crown did not follow Sepúlveda in his doctrine on just war against the Indians based on Aristotle could not be more specific or definitive than this declaration.

Writers outside of Spain have often described the Spanish conquest of America as primarily an enterprise marked by plunder and cruelty. That there was plunder and cruelty cannot be denied. But it is also true that Spain, in the very course of carving out her empire, was agitated for decades by her effort to rule justly. And if Spain was the only country which produced an articulate champion of the application of Aristotle's doctrine of natural slavery to the native peoples of its empire, she also produced his powerful opponent. The Spanish struggle for justice was deeply serious and bitterly fought, not a cynical gesture akin to the spirit of the Walrus in *Alice's Adventures in Wonderland* who held a hypocritical handkerchief before his streaming eyes while he greedily sorted out the innocent oysters "for those of the largest size".

It may take a long time to convince non-Spaniards of this, just as it will to persuade his countrymen that Las Casas was not a disloyal Spaniard.[53] The intense opposition aroused by his actions and his ideas has never ceased; even today some Spaniards denounce him. As recently as 1938, for example, a strong movement was set afoot to change the name of "Fray Bartolomé de Las Casas" street in Sevilla, and only by the energetic resistance of a Cabinet minister was his name preserved in a street of the city of his birth, where he was consecrated bishop of Chiapa, and where he published his nine formidable treatises which will be read and discussed as long as the history of Spain in America is studied.[54] As late as 1955, when it was proposed that Las Casas should be selected—because of his contributions to the laws of the Indies—as one of the jurists whose busts would grace the façade of the Faculty of Law of the University of Seville in its imposing new quarters, strong resistance was expressed and only after a lively battle was the proposal finally accepted.[55]

How can this persistent hostility to Las Casas be explained? His intemperance alienated many in his own time, and later too. His vehemence, his exaggeration, his unwillingness to sugar-coat the pill of his continuous and unpalatable criticism, and his incorrigible habit of speaking his mind freely to king, courtier, or conquistador roused much resentment. His central idea was itself shocking to many of his contemporaries. To practical conquistadores and administrators, men struggling for immediate worldly goals, and perhaps to the crown as well, jealous as it was of all royal prerogatives, his reiteration that the only justification for the presence of Spaniards in the New World was the Christianization of the Indians by patiently peaceful means alone seemed dangerous nonsense. What they must have felt when he declared that it would be better for the Spaniards to leave the New World, with its Indians un-Christianized, than to remain and to bring them into the fold by forcible, un-Christian methods is not difficult to imagine.

The Valladolid dispute remains an important part of the controversy which has always surrounded the figure of Las Casas, and no one writing on Spain in America can ignore it. But it lives on principally because of the universality of the ideas on the nature of man which Las Casas enunciated, when he set forth in dramatic and compelling fashion his doctrine that "all the peoples of the world are men" and his faith that God would not allow any nation to exist, "no matter how barbarous, fierce, or depraved its customs" which might not be "persuaded and brought to a good order and way of life, and made domestic, mild, and tractable, provided the method that is proper and natural to men is used; namely, love, gentleness, and kindness".

One of the finest passages in the Valladolid argument of Las Casas serves to illustrate the simple grandeur of which he was capable at his best:

"Thus mankind is one, and all men are alike in that which concerns their creation and all natural things, and no one is born enlightened. From this it follows that all of us must be guided and aided at first by those who were born before us. And the savage peoples of the earth may be compared to uncultivated soil that readily brings forth weeds and useless thorns, but has within itself such natural virtue that by labour and cultivation it may be made to yield sound and beneficial fruits."[56]

Las Casas was here arguing against Aristotle, but he was also stating a proposition which has rallied men in many parts of the world. And he was basing his argument on the belief that the way to civilize any people was to bring religion and education to them, and not just to accustom them to the material goods hitherto unknown to them. The recommendation of Bernardo de Gálvez in eighteenth-century Mexico that Indians were to be given "horses, cattle, mules, guns, ammunition, and knives" and were to be encouraged to "become greedy for the possession of land" would have been anathema to Las Casas.[57]

Las Casas may have been wrong in his bold declaration that "all the peoples of the world are men", if this is taken to mean equality in all things. Recent scientific investigations demonstrate that on the contrary men vary greatly in many of their physical and psychological characteristics.[58] But few today can be unmoved by his affirmation that "the law of nations and natural law apply to Christian and gentile alike,

and to all people of any sect, law, condition, or colour without any distinction whatsoever", or by the words in which
he set forth the sixth reason for the composition of his *History
of the Indies*:

"To liberate my own Spanish nation from the error and
very grave and very pernicious illusion in which they now
live and have always lived, of considering these people to lack
the essential characteristics of men, judging them brute beasts
incapable of virtue and religion, depreciating their good
qualities and exaggerating the bad which is in them. These
peoples have been hidden away and forgotten for many
centuries, and [it has been my purpose] to stretch out our
hands to them in some way, so that they would not remain
oppressed as at present because of this very false opinion of
them, and kept permanently down in the darkness."[59]

At a time when the conquistadores were bringing to the
notice of the European world a whole new continent in-
habited by strange races, it was Las Casas, rejecting Sepúlveda's view that the Indians were an inferior type of humanity
condemned to serve the Spaniards, who "stretched out his
hand" to the American Indians, with faith in the capacity for
civilization of all peoples. This conviction, in Las Casas and
other Spaniards, and the action which flowed from it, give a
unique distinction to the Spanish effort in America. Las Casas
represents both that "authentic Spanish fury" with which
Spaniards confront human and divine matters, and the typical
attitude of the Salamanca school of sixteenth-century theologians, who believed that thought and action must be so
intimately fused that they cannot be separated, and that
spiritual truths must be made manifest in the world about
us.[60] Las Casas thought that the end of the world might not
be far off—indeed, he wrote his *History of the Indies* in order to
explain God's action in the event that He decided to destroy
Spain for her misdeeds in America—but meanwhile there was

work to be done in the world. He would have agreed perfectly with the seventeenth-century Puritan Matthew Henry who declared: "The sons and daughters of heaven, while they are here in the world, have something to do about this earth, which must have its share of their time and thoughts."[61] He would also have considered as one of his followers Thomas Jefferson who wrote a few days before he died on July 4, 1826, "that the mass of mankind has not been born with saddles on their backs, nor a favoured few booted and spurred, ready to ride them legitimately, by the grace of God".[62]

It was Las Casas' determination to do something about the bodies and the souls of the American Indians that has made him one of the most popular folk-heroes of the New World. Simón Bolívar symbolized this feeling when he urged, during the days of the Angostura Congress in 1819, that the new revolutionary republic being established should be called Colombia, and its capital Las Casas. "Thus we will prove to the world", exclaimed the Liberator in one of his eloquent moments, "that we not only have the right to be free, but we will also demonstrate that we know how to honour the friends and benefactors of mankind. Columbus and Las Casas belong to America. Let us honour them by perpetuating forever their glorious achievements."[63]

Obviously, not all Spaniards who went to America followed the path of Las Casas, nor do all of their descendants there accept his ideas today. One twentieth-century Mexican writer has denounced the Indians as lazy, cruel, and drunken in the same spirit as his sixteenth-century forebears who considered them "dirty dogs" or "almost beasts".[64] Scholars are still to be found who sustain with "scientific" reasons the basic inferiority of certain races with the same fervour as Sepúlveda, but many more follow the ideas of Las Casas and revere him, as did Bolívar, as a "humane hero".[65]

Theories have practical application today, too, just as at the Valladolid dispute four hundred years ago. In Bolivia, for example, where agrarian reforms have been instituted to provide land for the Indians, a new social order seems to be emerging. Five years ago Indians were looked upon as "animal tillers of the soil". Today they drive tractors, have organized communal enterprises, and have demonstrated in many other small and large ways their capacity to develop and direct their own economic, social, and political affairs. Yet, here too, we find history repeating itself, for some members of the white and Spanish-speaking minority in Bolivia are still expounding the innate biological and cultural inferiority of the Andean Indian, who "can never be incorporated into the life of the nation".[66] Sepúlveda still is cited by unfriendly critics of Spain as one of the most shocking and blatant symbols of imperialism and colonialism, as may be seen from a recent attack published in the official organ of the Karl Marx University in the Soviet Zone of Germany.[67]

Despite the immense quantity of tendentious and propagandistic writing that has been ground out on the New World since Columbus first set sail, it is only sober truth that Portugal and Spain were the pioneers of the greatest expansion of Western civilization ever made. The South African historian Sidney R. Welch expressed it thus:

"They expanded the horizon and, therefore, potentially the domain of our Western Society from an obscure corner of the Old World, until it came to embrace all the habitable lands and navigable seas on the surface of the planet. It is owing to this Iberian energy and enterprise that Western Christendom has grown, like the grain of mustard seed in the parable, until it has become the Great Society."[68]

With this perspective, and taking into account the unsolved racial problems of today, we can see that the battle waged by Las Casas and by all those who sought to protect and educate the Indians is not yet won. But we can also see that the Valladolid controversy epitomized the problem for generations of men; it has today a larger significance than ever before. The whole world is involved today, not only the West. The United Nations Universal Declaration of Human Rights, adopted four centuries after Sepúlveda and Las Casas fought at Valladolid, proclaims that "All human beings are born free and equal in dignity and rights. They are endowed with reason and conscience and should act towards one another in a spirit of brotherhood."[69] If this be true, the decision of the Spanish crown and Council of the Indies not to stigmatize the American Indians as natural slaves, according to the dictates of Aristotle, becomes one of the milestones on the long road, still under construction, which slowly winds towards a civilization based on the dignity of man, that is to say, of all men.

APPENDIX A

The Exchange of Letters between Juan Ginés de Sepúlveda and Alfonso de Castro[1]

I. LETTER OF JUAN GINÉS DE SEPÚLVEDA TO ALFONSO DE CASTRO

Muy R^{do} padre

Mucho holgue quando v. m. me dixo q̃ [h]avia leido y considerado con diligencia el sumario de las quatro causas de mi libro por donde yo prueuo la conquista de las Indias ser justa y sancta haziendose con el temperamento q̃ se deue y los reies n[uest]ros tienen ordenado y mandan y quele [h]avia contentado y que por ellas yo prueuo bien mi intento. Despues desto vi el s[egun]do libro de la obra q̃ v. m. escriuio de punitione hereticorum adonde afirma lo mesmo en el cap. 14 donde v. m. prueua ser causa sufficiente de justa guerra la idolatria prouandolo por auctoridad dela sagrada scriptura donde añade estas palabras, *et testimonio huius* praecepti diuini fretus ego sentio iustum esse bellum q[uo]d catholici hispaniar[um] reges contra barbaras gentes idolatras, quae deum ignorabant versus occidens et austrum inuentas ante aliquot an[n]os gesserunt, et nunc etiam gerunt. Pero añade v. m. una condicion y es q̃ primero [h]an de ser amonestados q̃ se aparten dela idolatria, lo qual me haze mucha dificultad porq̃ esta admonicion ni la hizieron los judios a los amorrheos y a los otros moradores de la ti[er]ra de promission ni Gennadio de q̃ haze mencion Sant Gregorio, en la ep[istol]a 73 del p[ri]mer libro, ni los Reyes catholicos alos indios ni el papa alexandro en la bulla del decreto y concession q̃ les hizo manda q̃ se haga. Sup[li]co a v. m. me suelte esta dubda como esta lo uno con lo otro saluo si se dexo de hazer por ventura porq̃ considerandolo prudente-mente en todos estos lugares pareçio q̃ la admonestacion seria muy difficil o no aprouecharia nada porq̃ esta claro q̃ ninguna gente dexara la religion q̃ le dexaron sus passados sino por fuerça de armas o de milagros. Y q̃ en tal caso no se [h]a de hazer la admonicion inutil o difficil sino dexarla como sienten todos los theologos in correctione fraterna. asi q̃ se entienda q̃ entonces se [h]a de hazer la tal admonicion quando no fuere difficil o prudentemente se juzgare q̃ aprouechara q̃ desta manera pareçe q̃ no [h]aura contradicion y se satisfara a entrambas partes. Sup[li]co a v. m. q̃. en pocas palabras me responda a esto a las espaldas desta. Vale. non. julii.

Servidor de v[uest]ra m[erce]d
El doctor jo. sepulueda

II. Letter of Alfonso de Castro to Juan Ginés de Sepúlveda

Muy R^{do} señor

yo he mirado bien lo q̃ escreui enel libro 2 de iusta haereticorum punitione, cap. 14 y es verdad q̃ alli dixe q̃ antes q̃ se hiziesse guerra alos Indios era menester q̃ precediesse admonicion por la qual les admonestasen q̃ se apartasen de la idolatria q̃ tienen.[2] Esto dixe q̃ era necessario pa[ra] q̃ por esta admonicion constase dela p[er]tinacia q̃ ellos tienen en su maldad porq̃ contra aquel de quien no consta q̃ sea p[er]tinaz no me pareçe q̃ con iusto titulo se pueda hazer guerra. y por esta causa para q̃ conste de su p[er]tinacia dixe q̃ es menester q̃ preceda la tal admonicion porq̃ no la recebiendo quedara manifiesta su p[er]tinacia y obstinacion. Pero si por otra via por prudentes coniecturas pudiere aclararse la p[er]tinacia dellos sin q̃ preceda la tal admonicion, en tal caso digo q̃ iusta mente seles podra hazer guerra sinq̃ sean primero amonestados. y esto me pareçe conforme alo q̃ todos los theologos dizen de correctione fraterna[3] q̃ no obliga quando verisimilmente se cree q̃ no ha de aprovechar. Lo qual es conforme ala doctrina de sant pablo q̃ dize. Omnis qui arat, debet arare in spe fructus p[er]cipiendi. en lo de mas q̃ toca al sumario donde pone quatro razones para prouar su intento, yo digo q̃ lo vi y mire con diligencia, y me pareçio bien y doctamente puesto: et nihil inueni quod sit nigro carbone notandum. y porque estoi muy ocupado no digo mas de q̃ quedo

A seruicio de v[uest]ra m[erce]d
Fr. Alonso de Castro

APPENDIX B

Materials Used to Prepare this Study

1. *Manuscripts*

The principal sources bearing on the Valladolid dispute have been printed, except for the large Latin treatise, the "Apologia", by Las Casas. Even it may see the light soon; Ángel Losada, military attaché in the Spanish Legation in Switzerland, has started to transcribe the text and translate it into Spanish. When this difficult task has been completed and the work is published, we shall know the complete argument developed in 1550 by Las Casas. I did not use this MS. "Apologia"; for my purposes, Sepúlveda's position stood more in need of scrutiny than that of Las Casas which is well known.

Some few manuscripts from the great collection in the Archivo General de Indias are cited, but these are of relatively minor importance. The only significant unpublished new evidence comes from the exchange of letters between Sepúlveda and the Franciscan Alfonso de Castro which are printed here for the first time. The Peruvian Jesuit Rubén Vargas Ugarte discovered these letters and other material pertaining to the controversy in the library of the Convento de San Felipe in Sucre, Bolivia.[1] During work as a graduate student on a study of the political theories of Las Casas,[2] I came across a report on these manuscripts which had been brought together in a single volume entitled "Tratado de Indias de Monseñor de Chiapa y el Dr. Sepúlveda". I visited Sucre in the summer of 1935 on a Milton Fund grant from Harvard University and secured, through the kindness of the Rev. José Cuellar of the Convento, a photographic copy of the letters as well as of a *Relación* presented to the Council of the Indies in 1543 by Las Casas and his constant companion Friar Rodrigo de Ladrada.[3] In this long, impassioned indictment of Spanish cruelty to Indians the authors recommended that all licences to conquistadores be revoked and urged that the 1541 decision by Francisco de Vitoria, which insisted on adequate instruction of Indians before baptism, be promulgated and enforced. A close connection exists, then, between the *Relación* and the issues discussed in this essay.

Indeed, most of the documents in the volume in the Sucre archive bear on the Valladolid dispute. One, for example, summarizes the evidence taken down by the Jeronymite friars in 1517, while they served as administrators on the island of Hispaniola, on the question of the capacity of Indians to live like Spaniards.[4] Another is the retraction by the Dominican Domingo de Betanzos of his earlier declaration that the Indians were "beasts". Others are the much discussed regulations for confessing *encomenderos* and observations by Las Casas on the subject. Letters by the Indian defenders Sebastián Ramírez de Fuenleal and Tomás Casillas are also in the collection, together with résumés of the arguments at Valladolid and statements by Sepúlveda. Much of this material was used in the preparation of several of my earlier publications.

The letters in Appendix A did not strike me at first as particularly important or deserving of publication for, although they provided illustrations of Sepúlveda's position, it was not at that time the subject of dispute. When the new and, to me, startling interpretations by Losada, O'Gorman, and Quirk and the appearance in 1951 of Losada's edition of *Demócrates* forced me to examine anew the whole controversy, I re-studied my notes and encountered again the exchange of views between Sepúlveda and Castro. It was now evident that the letters constituted a small but capital piece of evidence on Sepúlveda's fundamental and apparently final views on waging war against the Indians. The letters have therefore become significant enough to print in Appendix A.

2. *Selected List of Printed Materials*

The items listed below were cited more than once in the course of the study.

Acosta, José de, *Obras del P. José de Acosta.* Francisco Mateos, ed. Madrid, 1954.

Bataillon, Marcel, *Erasmus en España.* 2 vols. Mexico, 1950.

—— "Novo mundo e fim do mundo", *Revista de História*, no. 18 (São Paulo, 1954).

—— "Pour l'"epistolario' de Las Casas. Une lettre et un brouillon", *Bulletin Hispanique*, LVI (Bordeaux, 1954), no. 4, 366–387.

Bejarano, Ignacio (Ed.), *Actas de cabildo de la ciudad de México.* 7 vols. Mexico, 1889–1900.

Bell, Aubrey F. G., *Juan Ginés de Sepúlveda.* Oxford, 1925.

Bernheimer, Richard, *Wild Men in the Middle Ages.* Cambridge—Mass., 1952.

Carro, Venancio D., *Domingo de Soto y su doctrina jurídica.* Second edition, Salamanca, 1944.

—— *La teología y los teólogos juristas españoles ante la conquista de América.* Second edition, Salamanca, 1951.

Ceccherelli, Claudio, "El bautismo y los franciscanos en México", *Missionalia Hispanica,* año XIII, no. 35 (Madrid, 1955).

Fabié, Antonio M., *Vida y escritos de don Fray Bartolomé de Las Casas.* 2 vols. Madrid, 1879.

Friede, Juan, "Las Casas y el movimiento indigenista en España y América en la primera mitad del siglo XVI", *Revista de Historia de América* (Mexico, 1952), no. 34, pp. 339–344.

Gerbi, Antonello, *Viejas polémicas sobre el nuevo mundo.* Lima, 1944.

Giménez Fernández, Manuel and Lewis Hanke (Eds.), *Bartolomé de Las Casas, 1474–1566. Bibliografía crítica y cuerpo de materiales para el estudio de su vida, escritos, actuación y polémicas que suscitaron durante cuatro siglos.* Santiago de Chile, 1954.

Hanke, Lewis, *The First Social Experiments in America.* Cambridge— Mass., 1935.

—— *La lucha por la justicia en la conquista de América.* Buenos Aires, 1949.

—— "Pope Paul III and the American Indian", *Harvard Theological Review,* XXX (1937), 65–102.

—— *The Spanish Struggle for Justice in the Conquest of America.* Philadelphia, 1949.

Hanke, Lewis, and Agustín Millares Carlo, eds., *Cuerpo de documentos del siglo XVI sobre los derechos de España en las Indias y Filipinas.* Mexico, 1943.

Kelemen, Pál, *Medieval American Art.* 2 vols. New York, 1943.

Las Casas, Bartolomé de, *Colección de tratados, 1552–1553.* Buenos Aires, 1924.

—— *Historia de las Indias.* Edited by Agustín Millares Carlo, with introduction by Lewis Hanke. 3 vols. Mexico, 1951.

Losada, Ángel, *Juan Ginés de Sepúlveda a través de su "Epistolario" y nuevos documentos.* Madrid, 1949.

—— (Ed.) *Juan Ginés de Sepúlveda. Demócrates segundo o de las justas causas de la guerra contra indios.* Madrid, 1951.

Manzano y Manzano, Juan, *La incorporación de las Indias a la corona de Castilla.* Madrid, 1948.

Martínez, Manuel María, "El obispo Marroquín y el franciscano Motolinía, enemigos de Las Casas", *Boletín de la Real Academia de la Historia,* CXXXII (Madrid, 1953), cuaderno 2.

Mateos, Francisco, S. J. (Ed.), *Obras del P. José de Acosta.* Madrid, 1954.

Medina, José Toribio, *Biblioteca hispanoamericana.* 7 vols. Santiago, 1897–1907.

Olarte, Teodoro, *Alfonso de Castro (1495–1558). Su vida, su tiempo y su ideas filosófico-jurídicas.* San José, Costa Rica, 1946.

Olschki, Leonardo, "Ponce de León's Fountain of Youth: A History of a Geographical Myth", *Hispanic American Historical Review*, XII (1941), 361–385.

d'Olwer, Luis Nicolau, *Fray Bernardino de Sahagún (1499–1590).* Mexico, 1952.

—— (Ed.) *Fray Toribio de Benavente (Motolinía). Relaciones de la Nueva España.* Mexico, 1956.

Phelan, John Leddy, *The Millennial Kingdom of the Franciscans in the New World. A Study of the Writings of Gerónimo de Mendieta (1526–1604).* Berkeley and Los Angeles, 1956. University of California Publications in History, Vol. 52.

Quirk, Robert E., "Some Notes on a Controversial Controversy: Juan Ginés de Sepúlveda and Natural Servitude", *Hispanic American Historical Review*, XXXIV (1954), 357–364.

Ricard, Robert, *La conquista espiritual de México.* Mexico, 1947.

Robles, Oswaldo, *Filósofos mexicanos del siglo XVI.* Mexico, 1950.

Rodríguez Villa, A., *Memorias para la historia del asalto y saqueo de Roma. . . .* Madrid, 1875.

Sauer, Carl O., *Agricultural Origins and Dispersals.* New York, 1952.

Schlaifer, Robert O., "Greek Theories of Slavery from Homer to Aristotle", *Harvard Studies in Classical Philology*, no. 47 (Cambridge—Mass., 1936), pp. 165–204.

Solórzano, Juan de, *Política indiana.* Madrid, 1647.

Welch, Sidney R., *Europe's Discovery of South Africa.* Cape Town and Johannesburg, 1935.

Notes

INTRODUCTION

1. Charles Jourdain, *De l'influence d'Aristote et de ses interprètes sur la découverte du nouveau monde* (Paris, 1861).
2. Juan Comas, *Racial Myths* (Paris, 1951), p. 7.
3. Melvin Conant, *Race Issues on the World Scene* (Honolulu, 1955), p. 130.

CHAPTER I

1. James Westfall Thompson, *Feudal Germany* (Chicago, 1928), pp. 401–402, 488–489.
2. Dominik Josef Wörfel, "La curia romana y la corona de España en la defensa de los aborígenes canarios", *Anthropos*, XXV (Vienna, 1930), 1011–1083. The Catalan mystic and missionary, Ramón Lull, may have been responsible for sending ecclesiastics to the Canary Islands and for the application there of peaceful conversion practices. This is the view sustained by Elías Serra Rafols in *La missió de R. Lull i els missioners mallorquins del segle XIV* (Mallorca, 1954), as reviewed in *Revista de Historia*, XX, nos. 105–108 (La Laguna de Tenerife, 1954), pp. 184–185. Joaquín Xirau points out the parallel between the ideas of Lull and Las Casas, "Ramón Lull y la utopia española", *Asomante* (Puerto Rico, 1945), no. 3, p. 43; no. 4, p. 45. The most recent study is by Ramón Sugranyes de French, *Raymond Lulle: Docteur des Missions* (Fribourg, 1954). It is interesting to note that Lull admitted "la possibilité de l'emploi de la force contre les infidèles—non pas pour les convertir, mais pour rendre possible la prédication" (p. 80).
3. Sidney R. Welch, *Europe's Discovery of South Africa* (Cape Town and Johannesburg, 1935), pp. 112–113, 148.
4. Referring to the Negro slaves brought back from Africa, Azurara stated: "... posto que os seus corpos stevessem em algũa sogeiçom, esto era pequena cousa em comparaçom das suas almas, que eternalmente avyam de possuyr verdadeira soltura", *Chronica do descrobrimento de Guiné*, chap. XIV. A recent study is Margarida Barradas Carvalho, "L'idéologie religieuse dans la *Crónica de Guiné*", *Bulletin des études portugaises et de l'Institut Français au Portugal*, nouv. ser., XIX (Lisbon,

1957), 34–63. When the Portuguese reached India, the situation was entirely different, for there they met Hindus and not the Moslems, against whom they were "to wage incessant war". Affonso de Albuquerque thus instructed Frei Luis to treat the Hindus well. H. Morse Stephens, *Albuquerque* (Oxford, 1897), pp. 65–66.

5. A goodly portion of this literature is referred to in a book review by Francis M. Rogers, *Boletim da Sociedade de Geografia de Lisboa*, LXXIII, nos. 7–9 (Lisbon, 1955), pp. 405–410.

6. Portuguese indifference has been studied at length by Fidelino de Figueiredo, "A epica portuguesa no seculo XVI: Subsidios documentares para uma theoria geral da epopêa", *Boletins da Faculdade de Filosofia, Ciências e Letras*, C 1. *Letras*, no. 6 (São Paulo, 1950), pp. 61ff. For Spanish restraint with respect to America, see Marcos A. Morínigo, *América en el teatro de Lope de Vega* (Buenos Aires, 1946), pp. 11–54. A useful summary may be found in Ángel Franco, *El tema de América en los autores españoles del siglo de oro* (Madrid, 1954). Philip II possessed very few objects of art depicting America in his vast collection, according to the *Inventario hecho al muerte de Felipe II* in the Museo del Prado. Sr. F. J. Sánchez Canton, director of the museum, was kind enough to show me this important document.

The French also displayed little interest in the New World, according to Geoffroy Atkinson, *Les nouveaux horizons de la Renaissance* (Paris, 1935). Twice as many books were printed on Turkey during the period 1480–1609 as on North and South America together. Ten times as many brochures on Turkish events were issued. Books on the East Indies and on Asia generally also surpassed those on America (pp. 10–11). Nor was Italy greatly excited, according to Rosario Romeo, *Le scoperte americane nella coscienza italiana del Cinquecento* (Milan-Naples, 1954).

7. Francisco López de Gómara, *Hispania Victrix. Primera y segunda parte de la Historia general de las Indias* (Saragossa, 1552). The statement appears in the first sentence of the dedication to Emperor Charles V and reads: "Muy soberano Señor: La mayor cosa después de la creación del mundo, sacando la encarnación y muerte del que lo crió, es el descubrimiento de Indias; y así, las llaman Mundo-Nuevo." See also Pedro Borges, "El sentido trascendente del descubrimiento y conversión de Indias", *Missionalia Hispanica*, XIII (Madrid, 1956), 141–177.

8. Luis Weckmann, "The Middle Ages in the Conquest of America", *Speculum*, XXVI (1951), no. 1, pp. 130–141. Claudio Sánchez-Albornoz has presented many suggestive ideas in his essay "La edad media y la empresa de América", in *España y el islam* (Buenos Aires, 1943), pp. 181–199. Lively and related studies are Irving A.

Leonard, "Conquerors and Amazons in Mexico", *Hispanic American Historical Review*, XXIV (1944), 561–579; Otis H. Green, "Notes on the Pizarro Trilogy of Tirso de Molina", *Hispanic Review*, IV (1936), 208–209; and Affonso Arinos de Mello Franco, *O indio brasileiro e a revolução francesa* (Rio de Janeiro, 1937). On the persistence of the legendary earthly paradise to be found in the Atlantic, see George Boas, *Essays on Primitivism and Related Ideas in the Middle Ages* (Baltimore, 1948), p. 172. George P. Hammond has recently demonstrated that fantastic ideas persisted long after the first century of conquest and that "these stories of the fabulous were an integral feature of the age of the discovery of America and the conquest of its native peoples", "The Search for the Fabulous in the Settlement of the Southwest", *Utah Historical Quarterly*, XXIV (1956), 19. One idea widely cherished was that St Thomas had christianized the New World centuries before. A German newsletter (*c.* 1514) reported that Indians met by the Portuguese in Brazil were eager to point out his footsteps in the hinterland. The Indians also suffered a strange fantasy concerning Europe, for the Portuguese returned with their ship below deck "laden with brazil wood and above deck full of purchased young boys and girls which cost the Portuguese little since most of them were offered voluntarily, for these people actually believe their children are travelling to the Promised Land". *Tidings out of Brazil*. Translated by Mark Graubard. Commentary and Notes by John Parker (Minneapolis, 1957), p. 34.

9. For general views, see Carmelo Viñas y Mey, "El espíritu castellano de aventura y empresa y la España de los Reyes Católicos", *Archivo del Derecho Público*, V (Granada, 1952), 13–83; Ida Rodríguez Prampolini, *Amadises en América. La hazaña de Indias como empresa caballeresca* (Mexico, 1948).

10. S. E. Morison, *The Second Voyage of Christopher Columbus from Cadiz to Hispaniola and the Discovery of the Lesser Antilles* (Oxford, 1939), pp. 91–94, gives an amusing account of the maritime adventures of these virgins.

11. Leonardo Olschki, "Ponce de León's Fountain of Youth: A History of a Geographical Myth", *Hispanic American Historical Review*, XXI (1941), 384. As late as 1528 Antonio de Villasante obtained the privilege of selling certain drugs he had discovered on the island of Hispaniola, one of which was a marvellous "oil which enabled one to avoid old age", José Pérez de Barradas, "De cómo los españoles descubrieron la medicina de los indios", *Boletín de la Real Academia de la Historia*, CXXV (Madrid, 1949), 260.

12. Luis Nicolau d'Olwer, *Fray Bernardino de Sahagún (1499–1590)* (Mexico, 1952), p. 144.

13. H. W. Janson, *Apes and Ape Lore in the Middle Ages and the*

Renaissance (London, 1952), pp. 74–75. See also Otis H. Green, "'Lo de tu abuela con el ximio' (*Celestina*, Auto 1)", *Hispanic Review*, XXIV (1956), 1–12.

14. *The Golden Land*, edited by Harriet de Onís (New York, 1948), pp. 7–8.

15. Richard Bernheimer, *Wild Men in the Middle Ages* (Cambridge—Mass., 1952), pp. 1–2, 20.

16. *Ibid.*, fig. 49.

17. *Ibid.*, p. 179.

18. Elizabeth Wilder Weismann, *Mexico in Sculpture* (Cambridge—Mass., 1950), fig. 19.

19. E. P. Goldschmidt, "Not in Harrisse", in *Essays Honoring Lawrence C. Wroth* (Portland, Maine, 1951), p. 140.

20. Wilberforce Eames, "Description of a Wood Engraving, Illustrating the South American Indians (1505)", *Bulletin of the New York Public Library*, XXXVI (September, 1922), no. 9, pp. 755–760.

21. *Ibid.*, p. 759.

22. On the Devil in Mexico and Central America, see Rafael Heliodoro Valle, "El diablo en Mesoamérica", *Cuadernos Americanos*, XII (Mexico, 1955), no. 2, pp. 194–208. See also Gustavo Correa, *El espíritu del mal en Guatemala* (New Orleans, 1955), pp. 48–52.

23. José Durand, *Ocaso de sirenas manatíes en el siglo XVI* (Mexico, 1950).

24. Enrique de Gandía, *Historia crítica de los mitos de la conquista americana* (Madrid, [1929]), Chap. 2. Other contributions on myths are: Robert Hale Shields, "The Enchanted City of the Caesars, Eldorado of Southern South America", *Greater America* (Berkeley, 1945), pp. 319–340; Demetrio Ramos, "Examen crítico de las noticias sobre el mito del Dorado", *Cultura Universitaria* (Caracas, 1954), no. 41, pp. 19–58; and Constantino Bayle, S.J., *El dorado fantasma* (Second ed., Madrid, 1943).

25. Pedro Cieza de León, *Parte primera de la chrónica del Perú* (1553), Chap. 52. Antonio Pigafetta, chronicler of Magellan's voyage, reported that they carried on a friendly conversation with a Patagonian giant so tall that their heads reached only to his waist. Francisco Encina, *Historia de Chile* (20 vols., Santiago, 1940–1952), I, 388. Encina goes on to say that Las Casas and other friars manifested an equally fantastic spirit when they thought the Indians were capable of civilization. *Ibid.*, I, 389.

26. Philip A. Means, *The Spanish Main* (New York, 1935), Chap. 5.

27. Olschki, *Ponce de León's Fountain of Youth*, p. 384.

28. W. R. Jackson, *Early Florida Through Spanish Eyes* (Miami, 1954), Introduction. A rich literature on unicorns is to be found in the Muslim

world, according to Richard Ettinghausen, *The Unicorn* (Washington, 1950).

29. Juan de Solórzano Pereira has collected much information on these possibilities, and tends to discount all such stories of previous knowledge of America as attempts by jealous foreign nations to diminish the glory of Spain, *Política indiana* (Madrid, 1647), Libro I, caps. VI–VII.

30. Additional information on these questions will be found in the writer's *The First Social Experiments in America* (Cambridge—Mass., 1935), and *The Spanish Struggle for Justice in the Conquest of America* (Philadelphia, 1949). Alberto Salas gives a summary of opposed opinions on the Indians by two early writers in his article "Pedro Mártir y Oviedo ante el hombre y las culturas americanas", *Imago Mundi*, I (Buenos Aires, 1953), no. 2, pp. 16–33. Europeans invented the "noble savage" concept, in accordance with their moral, political, and social ideas, before Indians were discovered, according to Giuseppi Cocchiara, *Il mito del buon selvaggio* (Messina, 1948), p. 7. Mircea Eliade accepts this explanation in part and then goes on to provide a psychological answer, "El mito del buen salvaje o los prestigios del origen", *La Torre*, año III, no. 11 (Universidad de Puerto Rico, 1955), 49–66. Neither view satisfies one who has worked in the Iberian sources, particularly the voluminous reports on contacts between Spaniards and Indians.

31. J. B. Trend, *The Civilization of Spain* (London, 1944), p. 88. What Nebrija stated in his introduction was: "siempre la lengua ha sido compañera del imperio".

32. Las Casas and his early support of Negro slavery has been a subject of perennial interest, especially to those who do not like Las Casas. For a well-written defence of Las Casas see Fernando Ortiz, "La leyenda negra contra Fray Bartolomé de Las Casas", *Cuadernos Americanos* (Mexico, 1952), no. 5, pp. 146–184. Marcel Bataillon gives a valuable brief note in "Le 'clerigo Casas' ci-devant colon, réformateur de la colonisation", *Bulletin Hispanique*, LIV (1952), 366–368.

33. The fundamental work by Alonso de Sandoval is *Natvraleza policia sagrada i profana, costvumbres i ritos disciplina i catechismo evangelico de todos etiopes* (Seville, 1627), and a popular item is by Mariano Picón Salas, *Pedro Claver. El santo de los esclavos* (Mexico, 1950). Neither Jesuit appears to have denounced Negro slavery as an un-Christian institution.

34. Archivo de Indias. Indiferente general 424, libro 22, f. 133. See also fs. 134–136; 152 vuelto—155; 219 vuelto—224 vuelto; 298 vuelto —299 vuelto; 334–335. Carlos A. Romero has written a brief account, "El camello en el Perú", *El Comercio* (Lima, 28 de febrero, 1937), and has also treated the subject in his *Los héroes de la isla de gallo* (Lima,

1945). Ricardo Cappa also gives some pertinent information in his *Estudios críticos acerca de la dominación española en América* (6 parts; Madrid, 1889–1897), V, 428, but the subject is a hilarious one and merits investigation.

CHAPTER II

1. Francisco Romero, *Sobre la filosofía en América* (Buenos Aires, 1952), p. 125. Marcel Bataillon has been working intensively in this field during the last few years and has given a summary of his 1951–1952 lectures on "La découverte spirituelle du Nouveau Monde" in the *Annuaire du Collège de France* (1952), pp. 276 ff.

2. Marcel Bataillon, "Novo mundo e fim do mundo", *Revista de História*, no. 18 (São Paulo, 1954), p. 350.

3. Welch, *Europe's Discovery of South Africa*, p. 249.

4. *Catálogo de pasajeros a Indias*, edited by Cristóbal Bermúdez Plata (3 vols., Seville, 1940–1946). An analytical article of value is by V. Aubrey Neasham, "Spain's Emigrants to the New World, 1492–1592", *Hispanic American Historical Review*, XIX (1939), 147–160.

5. Colección de Juan Bautista Muñoz, Academia de la Historia (Madrid), LXXX, 270. José Durand has begun to open up this subject in his useful work on *La transformación social del conquistador* (2 vols., Mexico, 1953). Some valuable references will be found in C. J. Bishko, "The Iberian Background of Latin American History: Recent Progress and Continuing Problems", *Hispanic American Historical Review*, XXXVI (1956), 67, note 31.

6. Bartolomé de Las Casas, *Historia de las Indias*, edited by Agustín Millares Carlo with introduction by Lewis Hanke (3 vols., Mexico, 1951), I, 472–473. Américo Castro remarks on the reluctance of Spaniards to work with their hands in *The Structure of Spanish History* (Princeton, 1954), pp. 631–632, but the topic has not yet been sufficiently studied. Another study by Castro is "Algunas observaciones acerca del concepto del honor en los siglos XVI y XVII", *Semblanzas y estudios españoles. Homenaje ofrecido a don Américo Castro por sus exalumnos de Princeton University* (Princeton, 1956), pp. 319–382. A beginning has been made by Alfonso García Valdecasas, *El hidalgo y el honor* (Madrid, 1948). In reviewing this work, José Durand has brought together some valuable ideas and bibliography, *Nueva Revista de Filología Hispánica*, IV (1950), 71–75. Julio Heise González has brought together a number of illustrations of the reluctance of Spaniards to perform manual labour in America in "Las tasas y ordenanzas sobre el trabajo de los indios en Chile", *Anales de la Universidad de Chile*, serie segunda, VII (1929), 821–823.

The first scientific treatise on agriculture in Spain includes a ringing statement in favour of labour on the land, and even a recommendation that those who are too lazy to work should be denied food or even killed. Gabriel Alonso de Herrera, *Libro de agricultura, que es de la labrança y criança, y de muchas otras particularidades y provechos del campo* (Valladolid, 1563), fol. 3v.

A basic work on Spanish character is by María Rosa Lida de Malkiel, *La idea de la fama en la edad media Castellana* (Mexico, 1952), and a related study is the article by José Luis Romero, "Sobre la biografía española del siglo XV y los ideales de vida", *Cuadernos de historia de España*, I–II (Buenos Aires, 1944), 114–138.

7. Delgado, *Historia general sacro-profana, política y natural de las islas del poniente llamadas Filipinas*, tomo único (Manila, 1892), p. 301.

8. Pedro Leturia, "Maior y Vitoria ante la conquista de América", *Estudios Eclesiásticos*, II (Madrid, 1932), 44–82. A more recent study is by Silvio Zavala as the introduction for the volume *De las islas del mar océano, por Juan López Palacios Rubios. Del dominio de los Reyes de España sobre los indios, por Fray Matías de Paz* (Mexico, 1954). Translation, notes, and bibliography by Agustín Millares Carlo.

9. Rafael Altamira, "El texto de las leyes de Burgos de 1512", *Revista de Historia de América* (Mexico, 1938), no. 4, pp. 5–79.

10. The writer has published two articles on this subject: "The Requirement and Its Interpreters", *Revista de Historia de América* (Mexico, 1938), no. 1, pp. 28–34; and "A aplicação do requerimiento na America Espanhola", *Revista do Brasil* (Rio de Janeiro, Sept., 1938), pp. 231–248. As Juan Manzano y Manzano has pointed out, Requirement ideas were informally put into practice earlier than 1512, *La incorporación de las Indias a la Corona de Castilla* (Madrid, 1948), p. 33. The Requirement still provokes discussion, as may be seen from Alfonso García Gallo, "El derecho común ante el Nuevo Mundo", *Revista de Estudios Políticos*, LIII, no. 80 (Madrid, 1955), 133–152.

11. The only description extant of this controversy comes from Las Casas, *Historia de las Indias*, Libro III, Chaps. 149–151. The courage displayed by Las Casas in opposing Aristotle may be appreciated in the light of the experience of Sepúlveda's master Pietro Pomponazzi of Bologna. The dogma of the Church had been based on Aristotle as interpreted by Thomas Aquinas. When Pomponazzi claimed the right to study Aristotle for himself, his 1516 treatise *De immortalitate animi* was burned at Venice and Pompanozzi ran serious risk of death at the hands of the Catholics. "Any attack on Aristotle, or even an attempt to reopen the old discussions on the Aristotelian problems was regarded as a dangerous heresy", according to John Malcolm Mitchell, *Encyclopedia Britannica* (Eleventh edition, 1911), XXII, 58. See also Andrew

Halliday Douglas, *The Philosophy and Psychology of Pietro Pomponnazi* (London, 1910). The *Politics* enjoyed in sixteenth- and seventeenth-century Spain a "respeto casi supersticioso", according to Antonio Domínguez Ortiz, "La esclavitud en Castilla durante la edad media", *Estudios de historia social de España* (2 vols., Madrid, 1952), II, 406. Aristotle was never used to justify slavery in medieval Spain or Portugal, as there was no real need to explain the enslavement of Moslems. For a thorough treatment, see Charles Verlinden, *L'Esclavage dans l'Europe médiévale. Tome premier. Peninsula Ibérique-France* (Bruges, 1955).

12. Sister Margaret Mary, C.I.M., "Slavery in the Writings of St Augustine", *The Classical Journal*, XLIX (1954), 367. José Almoina has collected many examples, however, to show that there was a definite attempt to establish a "conexión de la idea de libertad espiritual de las Sagradas Escrituras con el orden social". See pp. 170–175 of his edition of *Fray Juan de Zumárraga. Regla cristiana breve* (Mexico, 1951).

13. Herschel Baker, *The Dignity of Man* (Cambridge—Mass., 1947), p. 178.

14. The literature on Caribs is large, confusing, and somewhat contradictory. A valuable collection of manuscript material on the treatment of Caribs by Spaniards up to about 1520 is to be found in the third *legajo* of the *residencia* of Rodrigo de Figueroa in the Archivo de Indias, Justicia 47. This early ethnographic document describes the attempts made to determine which Indians captured by Spanish captains cruising along Tierra Firme and the islands actually were Caribs. An unpublished paper entitled "Los Caribes" has been prepared by Vicenta Cortés of the Archivo de Indias, in which reference is made to other manuscripts there on Spanish relations with Caribs in the sixteenth century.

Columbus was originally responsible for the idea that Caribs were cannibals, according to Gandía, *Mitos de la conquista*, p. 47. Julio C. Salas, in *Los indios caribes* (Madrid, 1920), states that the Caribs were a brave, intelligent race and not cannibalistic as was claimed by those desirous of enslaving them. Domínguez places the blame on the Latin translation of Columbus's letter to Luis de Santangel where the phrase *comer carne viva* was rendered as *carne humana vescuntur*, and concluded: "That barbarous Indians are treacherous; that when they slay their enemies they will tear them to pieces and burn them is beyond dispute. But that they will eat their flesh is a slander and a despicable falsehood founded on interested motives. I have yet to find the man who will tell me in good faith he has seen the Indians eat human flesh", *The Conquest of the River Plate, 1535–1555*, L. L. Domínguez, ed. (London, 1891), pp. xxxvii–xxxviii. Domínguez was preparing a historical account of this subject, which appears not to have been published. William Dampier also showed scepticism concerning the tales of cannibalism in the West Indies in his *A New Voyage Round the World* . . . (third edition corrected, London, 1698), pp. 485–486. Alexander von Humboldt and Aimé Bonpland thought the cannibalism of the inhabitants of the West Indies was much exaggerated, *Personal Narrative of Travels to the Equinoctial Regions of America During the Years 1799–1804*, edited by Thomasina Ross (3 vols., London, 1894), III, 86. Ewald Volhard gives a general view of the subject in *Kannibalismus* (Stuttgart, 1939), pp. 324–361.

Woodbury Lowery, *Spanish Settlements within the Present Limits of the United States* (New York, 1901), brings together some of the early Spanish legislation on Caribs on pp. 110–111. As a curious sidelight, Pedro Aguado tells us that some Indians in New Granada believed the Spaniards to be cannibals and thus fought desperately since they felt sure the invaders were looking for food, *Historia de Santa Marta y Nuevo Reino de Granada*, edited by Jerónimo Bécker (2 vols., Madrid, 1916–1917), II, 38–39.

Professor John H. Rowe of the University of California, Berkeley, writes: "There is no question that the Spaniards attributed cannibalism to many Indians who did not practice it in order to enslave them, but there nevertheless seems to be a good basis in fact for the attribution of cannibalism to *some* Caribs."

15. The letter is dated December 10, 1555, and is in Archivo de Indias, Lima 313.

16. The writer gives a fuller description in "The Contribution of Bishop Juan de Zumárraga to Mexican Culture", *The Americas*, V (Washington, D.C., 1949), 275–282.

17. For a fuller account see the writer's "Pope Paul III and the American Indians", *Harvard Theological Review*, XXX (1937), 65–102. A more recent study, emphasizing the juridical points involved, is by Alberto de la Hera, "El derecho de los indios a la libertad y a la fe. La bula 'Sublimis Deus' y los problemas indianos que la motivaron", *Anuario de la Historia del Derecho Español*, XXVI (Madrid, 1956).

18. Antonio M. Fabié, *Vida y escritos de don Fray Bartolomé de Las Casas* (2 vols., Madrid, 1879), I, 30.

19. Claudio Ceccherelli, O. F. M., "El bautismo y los franciscanos en México", *Missionalia Hispanica*, año XIII, no. 35 (Madrid, 1955), p. 213. The best general treatment of the subject is by Robert Ricard, "Enseñanza prebautismal y administración del bautismo", in *La conquista espiritual de México* (Mexico, 1947), pp. 185–204.

20. Bataillon, *Novo mundo e fim do mundo*, p. 348.

21. John L. Phelan, *The Millennial Kingdom of the Franciscans in the*

New World (Berkeley and Los Angeles, 1956), p. 121, note 23, and *passim.*

22. Silvio Zavala, *Ideario de Vasco de Quiroga* (Mexico, 1941).

23. The many curious ideas cherished by the friar Francisco de la Cruz, which led to his burning at the stake by the Inquisition in Lima in 1578, have been described by Bataillon, *Novo mundo e fim do mundo.*

24. Mr Bruno Pagliai of Mexico City owns this document and has generously permitted the writer to use it. It has been published, with notes, by Juan Mesaguer Fernández, "A Doubt of Some of the Franciscan Missionaries in Mexico Solved by Pope Paul III at the Request of Cardinal Quiñones", *The Americas*, XIV (1957), 183–189. Franciscans today are still agitated by the baptismal controversy in sixteenth-century Mexico, as may be seen from the somewhat apologetic and defensive tone of Father Ceccherelli in his learned exposition, *El bautismo y los Franciscanos en México.*

25. Manuel María Martínez, "El obispo Marroquín y el franciscano Motolinía, enemigos de Las Casas", *Boletín de la Real Academia de la Historia*, CXXXII (Madrid, 1953), Cuaderno II, p. 192. The famous 1555 letter by Motolinía to Charles V in which this dispute is described may be found in *Colección de documentos inéditos, relativos al descubrimiento, conquista y organización de las antiguas posesiones españoles de América y Oceanía, sacados de los archivos del reino, y muy especialmente del de Indias* (42 vols., Madrid, 1864–1884), VII, 262–263. Hereafter cited as *Documentos inéditos de América.* For a balanced view of the Motolinía-Las Casas dispute, see Luis Nicolau d'Olwer's introduction to his *Fray Toribio de Benavente (Motolinía). Relaciones de la Nueva España* (Mexico, 1956), pp. xlix–lv. Biblioteca del Estudiante Universitario, no. 72.

26. *Documentos inéditos de América*, VII, 268.

27. Martínez, *El obispo Marroquín y el franciscano Motolinía*, pp. 195–196.

28. Luis Nicolau d'Olwer, *Fray Toribio de Benavente*, pp. 185–193.

29. *Ibid.*, p. 65.

30. *Ibid.*, p. 195.

31. For basic information and references to the pertinent documentation to this question, see the volume prepared by the writer and Manuel Giménez Fernández, *Bartolomé de Las Casas, 1474–1566. Bibliografía crítica y cuerpo de materiales para el estudio de su vida, escritos, actuación y polémicas que suscitaron durante cuatro siglos* (Santiago de Chile, 1954), pp. 64–65. Cited henceforth as *Las Casas. Bibliografía crítica.*

32. *De Indis*, I, xxiii. The text used is the volume edited by Ernest Nys, *De Indis et de Juri Belli Relectiones* (Washington, 1917).

33. *Ibid.*, pp. 120 ff.

34. *Ibid.*, p. 127.

35. Victor O'Daniel, *Dominicans in Early Florida* (New York, 1930), pp. 100–101.

36. Valladolid, 1560. A detailed analysis and description of this work has recently been provided by Luis Jaime Cisneros, "La primera gramática de la lengua general del Perú", *Boletín del Instituto Riva-Agüero*, *1951–1952*, I (Lima, [1953]), 197–264.

37. See the writer's *Spanish Struggle for Justice*, p. 12.

38. Edmundo O'Gorman, "Sobre la naturaleza bestial del indio americano", *Filosofía y Letras* (Mexico, 1941), no. 1, pp. 141–158; no. 2, pp. 305–315; and Alfonso García Gallo, *Revista de Estudios Políticos*, XXXIV (Madrid, 1950), 212–220. García Gallo considers that Betanzos used *bestia* only in a "sentido despectivo" and that Paul III's declaration that they were "truly men" demonstrates that they had been considered as men, though "incapaces". The reasoning becomes rather fine on this point!

39. Jerónimo de Mendieta, *Historia eclesiástica indiana*, edited by Joaquín García Icabalceta (Mexico, 1870), pp. 631–632.

40. See the writer's *First Social Experiments in America*, pp. 68–69.

41. Silvio Zavala, "Nuño de Guzmán y la esclavitud de los indios", *Historia Mexicana* (1952), no. 3, p. 413.

42. *History of the New World by Girolamo Benzoni of Milan*, edited by W. H. Smyth (London, 1857), p. 146.

43. *Ibid.*, p. 253.

44. Carl Lumholtz, *Unknown Mexico* (2 vols., New York, 1902), II, 470.

45. José María Vargas, *Fr. Domingo de Santo Tomás. Escritos* (Quito, 1937), p. 6.

CHAPTER III

1. References to material on this hectic phase of Las Casas' life will be found in *Las Casas, Bibliografía crítica*, pp. 101–120.

2. Letter of Tomás López Medel to the king, dated March 18, 1551. This valuable and interesting report has been published by Manuel Serrano y Sanz, "Algunos escritos acerca de las Indias, de Tomás López Medel", *Erudición Ibero-Ultramarina*, I (Madrid, 1930), 487–497.

3. Much information on ill treatment of friars is to be found in "Autos e informaciones por Diego Ramírez", Archivo de Indias, Justicia 331.

4. What little is known on the 1546 junta has been collected by Joaquín García Icazbalceta, *Don Fray Juan de Zumárraga* (Mexico, 1881), pp. 184 ff. The doctrines on peaceful preaching of Las Casas evidently

were fairly well known to his contemporaries. Robert S. Chamberlain has published a memorial of 1537–1538 showing that one of the Indian protectors was influenced by it, "Un documento desconocido del licenciado Cristóbal de Pedraza, protector de los indios y obispo de Honduras", *Anales de la Sociedad de geografía e historia de Guatemala*, XX (1945), 33–38.

5. The document is dated October 7, 1548. Archivo de Indias, México, 1841.

6. The cabildo of Santiago to the king, dated March 12, 1552. *Ibid.*, Guatemala 41. Two *legajos* of material on perpetuidad, largely unexploited, are in the Archivo de Indias, Indiferente General 1530 and 1624. Photographic copies of this rich collection have been deposited in the Library of Congress by the Carnegie Institution of Washington.

7. Juan Friede, "Las Casas y el movimiento indigenista en España y América en la primera mitad del siglo XVI", *Revista de Historia de América* (1952), no. 34, pp. 339–344.

8. Carta de don Luis de Velasco a Fr. Bartolomé de Las Casas, dated at Cholula, August 24, 1550. Academia de la Historia (Madrid). Colección Muñoz, tomo 85, fol. 330 vuelto.

9. Fr. Domingo de Santa María to Las Casas, dated at Coyoacán, July 7, 1549, *Documentos inéditos de América*, VIII, 204–206.

10. Archivo de Indias, Indiferente General 424, Libro 21, fol. 324.

11. *Ibid.*, México 1089, Libro 4, fol. 271. Real cédula dated at Valladolid, August 4, 1550. "Viejo y quebrantado" is the phrase used.

12. Luciano Pereña Vicente, "La soberanía de España en América", *Revista Española de Derecho Internacional*, V (Madrid, 1952), 893–924.

13. Cano opposed Sepúlveda as early as 1546 in lectures at the University of Alcalá. Maldonado's petition is in Bibliothèque Nationale (Paris). MS. Esp. no. 325, fols. 315–315 vuelto.

14. Otis H. Green, "A Note on Spanish Humanism. Sepúlveda and his Translation of Aristotle's Politics", *Hispanic Review*, VIII (1940), 339.

15. *Ibid.*, p. 340.

16. *Historia de la provincia de S. Vicente de Chyapa y Guatemala de la orden de Padre Sancto Domingo* (Madrid, 1619).

17. Marcel Bataillon attacks the Remesal story with zest and skill in his brilliant and absorbing article "La Vera Paz. Roman et histoire", *Bulletin Hispanique*, LIII (1951), 235–300. One gets the impression that Bataillon is so much engaged in demolishing the Remesal account that he does perhaps less than full justice to the real accomplishments of the Dominicans in Vera Paz. And of course adequate documentation has not yet been found to describe what actually happened. The letter sent by the Dominican Pedro de Angulo dated February 19, 1542, and not

mentioned by Bataillon, seems to refer to earlier achievements at peaceful preaching which tends to weaken somewhat the story as he presents it. The letter is in Archivo de Indias, Guatemala 168.

Remesal must be used with caution, of course—Padre Manuel María Martínez, O.P., of Madrid, in a letter dated Jan. 9, 1956, to the writer, points out that the common assumption that Las Casas studied at Salamanca is "una afirmación gratuita de Remesal". Manuel Giménez Fernández has published an important study, "La juventud en Sevilla de Bartolomé de Las Casas (1474–1502)", *Miscelánea de estudios dedicados a Fernando Ortiz*, II (La Habana, 1956), 671–717.

As an example of the complexity and difficulty of the subject may be cited the unpublished senior essay prepared at Princeton University in 1953 by Oliver Grant Bruton, "The Debate Between Bartolomé de Las Casas and Juan Ginés de Sepúlveda Over the Justice of the Spanish Conquest in America: Spain, 1550". Bruton believes that Bataillon has proved that the whole Vera Paz affair "was nothing more than a clever piece of propaganda used by Las Casas at the court to establish his idea of peaceful conversion" (p. 91).

18. *Las Casas. Bibliografía crítica*, pp. 100–107.

19. William H. Prescott, *The Conquest of Peru*, Book IV, Chap. 9.

20. "Pour l''epistolario' de Las Casas. Une lettre et un brouillon", *Bulletin Hispanique*, LVI (1954), 366–387. Bataillon's paleographical skill and deep knowledge of the period have enabled him to provide a readable text of the letter and to explain its significance.

21. *Ibid.*, p. 385.

22. *Ibid.*, p. 387.

23. Roberto Levillier, *Organización de la iglesia y las órdenes religiosas en el virreinato del Perú en el siglo XVI* (2 vols., Madrid, 1919), II, 68–69.

24. *The Structure of Spanish History* (Princeton, 1954), p. 190.

CHAPTER IV

1. The account given here is based on the writer's *Spanish Struggle for Justice*, Chap. 8.

2. Some impression of the great variety of opinions extant on Vitoria may be obtained from Teodoro Andrés Marcos, *Vitoria y Carlos V en la soberanía hispano-americana*, second ed. (Salamanca, 1946).

3. Venancio de Carro, *La teología y los teólogos juristas españoles ante la conquista de América*, second ed. (Salamanca, 1951), pp. 561–673. This fundamental work provides a detailed and searching examination of the theological aspects of the struggle at Valladolid. Other valuable general

works are Silvio Zavala's *Servidumbre natural y libertad cristiana según los tratadistas de los siglos XVI y XVII* (Buenos Aires, 1944) and his *La filosofía política en la conquista de América* (Mexico-Buenos Aires, 1947); and Joseph Höffner, *Cristentum und Menschenwürde—das Angliegen der spanischen Kolonialethik im Goldenen Zeitalter* (Trier, 1947). Of special use for the Valladolid controversy is Zavala's article, "Las Casas ante la doctrina de la servidumbre natural", *Revista de la Universidad de Buenos Aires*, año II (1944), 45–58.

4. Copies of the 1552 summary were distributed widely in the Indies, and were even to be found in Manila libraries, according to Jesús Gayo, O. P., "Rarezas bibliográficas en la Biblioteca de la Universidad de Santo Tomás", *Unitas*, XXVIII (Manila, 1955), 184–192.

5. For a list of the many editions and translations see *Las Casas. Bibliografía crítica*, pp. 146–147. The basic edition of Sepúlveda is *Demócrates segundo o de las justas causas de la guerra contra los indios*. Edición crítica bilingüe, traducción castellana, introducción, notas e índices por Ángel Losada. Madrid, 1951. Instituto Francisco de Vitoria. (Henceforth cited as *Demócrates*.) For an exhaustive treatment of the texts of treatises written by Sepúlveda on war against the Indians, see the Introduction to this work and another work by Losada, *Juan Ginés Sepúlveda a través de su "Epistolario" y nuevos documentos* (Madrid, 1949), pp. 651–656. Marcelino Menéndez Pelayo first published the treatise, with a Spanish translation and a brief introduction, in the *Boletín de la Real Academia de la Historia*, XXI (Madrid, 1892), 251–369. This edition was reprinted in Mexico under the title *Tratado sobre las justas causas de la guerra contra los indios* (1941), with a lengthy introduction by Manuel García-Pelayo entitled "Juan Ginés de Sepúlveda y los problemas jurídicos de la conquista de América" (pp. 1–42).

Information on the Valladolid dispute has been available in English since 1603 when Samuel Purchas published "The summe of the disputation betweene Fryer Bartolomew de las Casas or Casaus, and Doctor Sepúlveda", *Hakluytus Posthumus or Purchase His Pilgrimes*, MacLehose edition (Glasgow, 1906), XVIII, 176–180. Today, thanks to the activity of Dr Richard Morse, newly translated extracts of the views of both disputants are available in *Introduction to Contemporary Civilization in the West*, second edition (Columbia University Press, New York, 1954), I, 489–511.

CHAPTER V

1. *Demócrates*, pp. 19–25.
2. *Ibid.*, p. 22.
3. *Ibid.*, pp. 34–35.

4. Roger B. Merriman, *The Rise of the Spanish Empire in the Old World and the New* (4 vols., New York, 1918–1934), III, 346.

5. A. Rodríguez Villa, *Memorias para la historia del asalto y saqueo de Roma* ... (Madrid, 1875), pp. 121–122. For the large bibliography on this event, see Benito Sánchez Alonso, *Fuentes de la historia española e hispanoamericana* (third edition, 3 vols., Madrid, 1952), II, nos. 5502–5522.

6. Rodríguez Villa, *Memorias para saqueo de Roma*, p. 203. See also the translation with notes by John E. Longhurst, *Alfonso de Valdés and the Sack of Rome* (Albuquerque, 1952).

7. Marcel Bataillon, *Erasmo en España* (2 vols., Mexico, 1950), I, 477.

8. *Demócrates*, pp. 35–43.

9. *Psicología del pueblo español* (second edition, Barcelona, [1917]), p. 89. It may be pertinent to point out here that the belief that barbarians were by nature fitted only for slavery arose in the fifth century B.C. as a result of the intensification of nationalism that developed after the Persian wars, Robert O. Schlaifer, "Greek Theories of Slavery from Homer to Aristotle", *Harvard Studies in Classical Philology* (Cambridge—Mass., 1936), pp. 167–169, 201–202.

10. This citation comes from James T. Adams, *The Founding of New England* (Boston, 1927), pp. 14–15.

11. Pál Kelemen, *Medieval American Art* (2 vols., New York, 1943), I, 3. This work is well illustrated and provides much information on Indian artistic achievements. J. Eric S. Thompson, *The Rise and Fall of Maya Civilization* (Norman, Oklahoma, 1954), gives an up-to-date statement on what he describes as a remarkable genius in mathematics. Victor Wolfgang von Hagen has been investigating Inca roads and recently published a popular treatment, *Highway of the Sun* (New York, 1955). For a comparison of Spanish and Indian culture at the time of the conquest, Bailey W. Diffie in *Latin American Civilization* (Harrisburg, Penn., 1945) provides a useful antidote to some of the overly enthusiastic appraisals of Indian culture. He probably has not said the last word, however.

12. Zorita, "Breve y sumaria relación de los señores y maneras y diferencias que había de ellos en la Nueva España", in *Documentos inéditos de América*, II, 78 ff. Joaquín Ramírez Cabañas emphasizes in his edition of the *Relación* (Mexico, 1942), pp. vii–ix, how much Zorita supported Las Casas in his basic approach to Indian problems. Some of the early Franciscans also enquired why Indians were called "incapaces", given their sumptuous buildings, many skilled craftsmen, skill in speaking, courtesy in manners, and other accomplishments. Salvador Escalante Plancarte, *Fray Martín de Valencia* (Mexico, 1945), apéndice, p. xvi.

13. *Documentos inéditos de América*, II, 81.

14. Petition CXXV of the Cortes of 1548 gives point to Zorita's charge that Spaniards also showed ignorance of true values: "Iten es notorio el gran daño que estos reynos resciben por las buxerias, y vidrios, y muñecas y cuchillos, y naypes, y dados y otras cosas semejantes que vienen a estos reynos y se traen de fuera de ellos, como si fuesemos Indios, y por esta via sacan los que los traen gran negocio de dineros, sin dexar cosa provechosa para la vida humana, y que no sirve sino de niñerías y efectos." *Cortes de los antiguos reinos de León y de Castilla* (5 vols., Madrid, 1861–1903), V, 426.

15. See the writer's *Pope Paul III and the American Indians*, p. 79.

16. Ferdinand Denis, *Une fête bresilienne célébrée à Rouen en 1550* (Paris, 1850).

17. *Las Casas. Bibliografía crítica*, p. xix.

18. *Ibid.*, pp. 171–172.

19. Carl O. Sauer, *Agricultural Origins and Dispersals* (New York, 1952), pp. 42–43.

20. *Medieval American Art*, I, 3. For an up-to-date statement on the skill of Indians in working metals, with an abundant bibliography, see Dudley T. Easby, Jr., "Orfebrería y orfebres precolombinos", *Anales del Instituto de Arte Americano e Investigaciones Estéticas*, IX (Buenos Aires, 1956), 21–35.

21. Cited by Alexander von Humboldt, *Political Essay on New Spain* (2 vols., New York, 1811), II, 127, 161.

22. Héctor Ortiz D., "Bernal Díaz ante el indígena", *Historia Mexicana*, V (1955), no. 2, pp. 233–239.

23. *Demócrates*, p. 79.

24. *Ibid.*, pp. 78–79.   25. *Ibid.*, p. 79.

26. Luis Villoro, *Los grandes momentos del indigenismo en México* (Mexico, 1950), p. 25.

27. Sauer, *Agricultural Origins and Dispersals*, pp. 57–58.

28. Gerbi has published two fundamental works, *Viejas polémicas sobre el nuevo mundo* (Lima, 1944), and *La disputa del Nuovo Mundo; Storia di una polemica, 1750–1900* (Milan—Naples, 1955).

29. The manuscript is in the Bibliothèque Nationale (Paris) and is being transcribed and translated into Spanish by Ángel Losada. A photographic copy of the manuscript is in the Library of Congress.

30. This section is based on the writer's *Bartolomé de Las Casas. An Interpretation of His Life and Writings* (The Hague, 1951), pp. 61–89. Another recent analysis of the *Apologética historia*, from a particular point of view, has been made by Enrique Alvarez López, "El saber de la naturaleza en el padre Las Casas", *Boletín de la Real Academia de la Historia*, CXXXII (1953), 201–229.

31. A new edition of this work is badly needed today. A detailed index should be prepared by a trained anthropologist, so that the mass of information on Indian culture will be readily available.

32. Frank Tannenbaum has some cogent remarks on the problem, in so far as it affects Negroes, in "The Destiny of the Negro in the Western Hemisphere", *Political Science Quarterly*, XLI (March, 1946), no. 1, p. 41.

33. Aubrey F. G. Bell, "Spain's Attitude Toward the Renaissance", *Revista de Historia*, XV (Lisbon, 1926), 124–126.

34. Paul Oskar Kristeller, "Renaissance Philosophies", in *A History of Philosophical Systems*, edited by Vergilius Ferm (New York, 1950), p. 227.

35. Paul Oskar Kristeller, "Humanism and Scholasticism in the Italian Renaissance", *Byzantion*, XVII (1944–1945), 369–370. See also Kristeller's most recent study, *The Classics and Renaissance Thought* (Cambridge—Mass., 1955), Chap. II, on "The Aristotelian Tradition". As an indication of the popularity of Aristotle during the period in which Sepúlveda and Las Casas were active, it has been stated that "During the period 1526 to 1550, we find 116 editions of the works of Aristotle, of which 64 were published at Paris." Linton C. Stevens, "The Critical Appreciation of Greek Literature in the French Renaissance", pp. 147–161 in *South Atlantic Studies for Sturgis E. Leavitt*, edited by Thomas B. Stroup and Sterling A. Stoudemire (Washington, D. C., 1953), pp. 148–149.

36. Luis Nicolau d'Olwer, *Fray Bernardino de Sahagún*, p. 85.

37. *Obras del P. José de Acosta*, Francisco Mateos, ed. (Madrid, 1954), p. 47. The importance of Acosta's independent and scientific spirit has been described by Theodore Hornberger, "Acosta's *Historia Natural y Moral de las Indias*: A Guide to the Source and Growth of the American Scientific Tradition", *Studies in English, 1939* (University of Texas, 1939), pp. 139–162. Edmundo O'Gorman remarks on Acosta's reverence for Aristotle in the introduction to his edition of the *Historia natural y moral de las Indias* (Mexico, 1940), pp. xxxvi–xl.

38. John Tate Lanning, "The Reception of the Enlightenment in Latin America", in *Latin America and the Enlightenment*, edited by Arthur P. Whitaker (New York, 1942), p. 78.

39. Joaquín García Icazbalceta, *Bibliografía mexicana del siglo XVI*, edited by Agustín Millares Carlo (Mexico, 1954), p. 117.

40. Lester H. Rifkin, "Aristotle on Equality: A Criticism of A. J. Carlyle's Theory", *Journal of the History of Ideas*, XIV (1953), 276–283.

41. John S. Marshall, "Aristotle and the Agrarians", *The Review of Politics*, IX (1947), 352–354.

42. Charles J. O'Neil, "Aristotle's Natural Slave Reexamined", *The*

New Scholasticism, XXVII (1953), 247–279. The quotation appears on p. 279.

43. Some idea of the literature available may be seen from the review by Manuel Jiménez de Parga, "Los estudios de historia de la teoría política en los últimos cuatro años (1950–1954)", *Revista de Estudios Políticos* (Madrid, 1954), no. 75, pp. 213–258. Aristotelian references are particularly on pp. 249–258. A new edition of the original text with Spanish translation of the *Politics* was brought out recently by the Instituto de Estudios Políticos, *Aristóteles. Política*, Julián Marías and María Araujo, eds. (Madrid, 1951).

44. Schlaifer, *Greek Theories of Slavery from Homer to Aristotle*, pp. 188–189.

45. For O'Gorman's statement and discussion regarding it, see the writer's "Bartolomé de Las Casas: An Essay in Historiography and Hagiography", *Hispanic American Historical Review*, XXXIII (1953), 136–151.

46. Oswaldo Robles, *Filósofos mexicanos del siglo XVI* (Mexico, 1950), pp. 124–130, opposes O'Gorman's view of the Cartesian elements in Las Casas' thought. See also Phelan, *The Millennial Kingdom of the Franciscans in the New World*, pp. 62–63, 134.

47. Robert E. Quirk, "Some Notes on a Controversial Controversy: Juan Ginés de Sepúlveda and Natural Servitude", *Hispanic American Historical Review*, XXXIV (1954), 357–364. Quirk did not use the 1951 Losada text but the older and less complete version, which may explain some of his interpretations.

48. Aubrey F. G. Bell, *Juan Ginés de Sepúlveda* (Oxford, 1925), gives the essential biographical facts. A more recent and much more detailed treatment, the result of much labour in archives and libraries, is Losada's *Juan Ginés de Sepúlveda a través de su "Epistolario" y nuevos documentos.*

49. *Demócrates*. See the index for the many citations to Aristotle. In general, they all reflect Sepúlveda's conviction that he is "el mejor filósofo de todos" (pp. 12–13). Other similar expressions by Sepúlveda have been brought together by Marcial Solano, *Historia de la filosofía* (2 vols., Madrid, 1941), II, 33.

50. *Demócrates*, p. 121.

51. Losada, *Juan Ginés de Sepúlveda a través de su "Epistolario"*, pp. 100–101. At the age of eighty, Sepúlveda was still quoting Aristotle, Bell, *Juan Ginés de Sepúlveda*, p. 54.

52. *Demócrates*, pp. 20–22, 37–43.

53. Quirk, *Notes on a Controversial Controversy*, p. 358.

54. Julio Casares Sánchez, Secretary of the Real Academia Española, was kind enough to make available the relevant cards. Rafael Altamira

noted that *siervo* was equivalent to *esclavo* according to the Academy, in his *Diccionario castellano de palabras jurídicas y técnicas tomadas de la legislación indiana* (Mexico, 1951), p. 302. Though the question of the meaning of the Latin word *sclavus* did not arise in the Valladolid controversy, it may be useful to refer here to the detailed article by Charles Verlinden, "L'origine de sclavus= esclave", *Archivum Latinitatis Medii Aevi*, XVII (Brussels, 1942), 97–128. Sclavus was introduced in Spain in the thirteenth century, and became common usage in the fourteenth (pp. 117–119).

55. Bernard Weinberg, "From Aristotle to Pseudo-Aristotle", *Comparative Literature*, V (1953), 97–104.

56. Tomás and Joaquín Carrera y Artau, *Historia de la filosofía española. Filosofía cristiana de los siglos XIII al XV* (2 vols., Madrid, 1939–1943), II, 628–629.

57. Quirk, *Notes on a Controversial Controversy*, pp. 362–363.

58. *Demócrates*, pp. 122–123.

59. *Ibid.*, pp. 19–22.

60. Bede Jarrett, *Social Theories of the Middle Ages* (London, 1926), p. 103.

61. Conor Martin, "Some Medieval Commentaries on Aristotle's Politics", *History*, new series, XXXVI (London, 1951), 29–44.

62. Manuel García-Pelayo, in his introductory essay for the 1941 edition of Sepúlveda's treatise (see note 5, p. 136), spells out in detail on pp. 20–23 the dependence of Sepúlveda on Aristotle's doctrine of natural slavery by printing their texts in parallel columns.

CHAPTER VI

1. *Demócrates*, p. 29.

2. *Ibid.*, p. 31.

3. A succinct biography of Castro is given by Constancio Gutiérrez, *Españoles en Trento* (Valladolid, 1951), pp. 37–51. For his ideas, see Marcial Solano, *Los grandes escolásticos españoles de los siglos XVI y XVII: sus doctrinas filosóficas y su significación en la historia de la filosofía* (Madrid, 1928), pp. 70–88.

4. Teodoro Olarte, *Alfonso de Castro (1495–1558). Su vida, su tiempo y sus ideas filosófico-jurídicas* (San José, Costa Rica, 1946), p. 267. In an opinion of 1553, Castro raised some questions on the proposed sale of 2,300 Negroes in the Indias. F. Cerecedo, ed., "Un asiento de esclavos para América el año 1553, y parecer de varios teólogos", *Missionalia Hispanica*, III (Madrid, 1946), 580–597. On p. 588 there is a biographical and bibliographical note on Castro.

5. Olarte, *Alfonso de Castro*, pp. 22–23, 274.

6. "Parecer del Muy Reverendo Padre Fray Alonso de Castro, de la orden de San Francisco, cerca de dar los yndios perpetuos del Perú a los encomenderos", *Anuario de la Asociación Francisco de Vitoria*, IV (Madrid, 1933), 238–243. Castro opposes Las Casas' proposal to abolish all encomiendas on the grounds that this drastic action would lead to revolts in the Indies and would mean that the Indians would not be Christianized. He favours granting Indians, even in perpetuity, because the Spaniards would then have a compelling reason to preserve the Indians and protect them.

7. As translated by R. B. Cunninghame-Graham in his *Pedro de Valdivia. Conqueror of Chile* (London, 1926), pp. 194–195. The original text of Valdivia's letter of October 15, 1550, in which this statement appears, is given in *Cartas de Pedro de Valdivia* . . . , edited by José Toribio Medina (Sevilla, 1929), pp. 147–215. The quoted material is on p. 204. On the question of just war in Chile, see the recent solid monograph by Andrés Huneeus Pérez, *Historia de las polémicas de Indias en Chile durante el siglo XVI, 1536–1598* (Santiago, [1956]).

8. *Demócrates*, p. 63.

9. Las Casas, *Colección de tratados, 1552–1553* (Buenos Aires, 1924), pp. 134–135.

10. *Demócrates*, pp. 72–73.

11. See *Las Casas. Bibliografía crítica*, pp. 108–109, for the correspondence and relations between Cáncer and Las Casas at the time of this ill-fated missionary expedition to Florida. In 1558, after Ferrer had also perished in an attempt to preach the faith peacefully, Las Casas still supported this method. The Dominican provincial in Mexico, Fr. Domingo de Santa María, opposed further attempts, but Philip II and the Council heeded Las Casas and Fr Domingo de la Anunciación. J. Salvador y Conde, "El padre Domingo de la Anunciación y su personalidad misionera", *Missionalia Hispanica*, VII (Madrid, 1950), 118–120.

12. *Demócrates*, p. 73.

13. *Ibid.*, pp. 87 ff.

14. *Ibid.*, pp. 92–177 are published by Losada for the first time except pp. 98–99.

15. *Ibid.*, p. 96.

16. *Ibid.*, p. 101.

17. *Ibid.*, pp. 117–124.

18. *Ibid.*, pp. 119–121.

19. *Ibid.*, p. 121.

20. *Supra*, pp. 67–69.

21. *Demócrates*, pp. 122–123.

22. *Ibid.*, p. 124.

23. J. H. Parry used this phrase in a book review in the *English Historical Review*, LXVII (1952), 408.

24. Carro, *Teología y la conquista de América*, p. 617.

25. Quirk, *Notes on a Controversial Controversy*, p. 364.

26. See n. 6, p. 134. Marvin Goldwert has recently published an article in *Revista Histórica* (Lima) on the perpetuity question in Peru which utilizes some of this material.

27. *Las Casas. Bibliografía crítica*, p. 139.

CHAPTER VII

1. The standard work on this important theologian is by Venancio D. Carro, *Domingo de Soto y su doctrina jurídica* (second edition, Salamanca, 1944). His ideas still attract students, as may be seen by the dissertation by Salomón Rahaim, S.J., "Valor moral-vital del *De Iustitia et Jure* de Domingo de Soto, O.P.", *Archivo Teológico Granadino*, XV (Granada, 1952), 5–213.

Marcel Bataillon feels that Soto tried to remain aloof from the controversies over America, *Pour l'*"*epistolario*" *de Las Casas*, p. 373.

2. Archivo de Indias, Indiferente General 1530.

3. Ramón Riaza, "El primer impugnador de Vitoria: Gregorio López", *Anuario de la Asociación Francisco de Vitoria*, III (Madrid, 1932), 105–113. It should be remembered that López had been sent to Sevilla in 1543 to make a special investigation on "the liberty of the Indians" which yielded much information on their ill-treatment by Spaniards. Archivo de Indias, Patronato 185, ramo 24 and Patronato 231. This evidence has been printed, "Informaciones coloniales sobre libertad y tratamiento de los indios", *Revista del Archivo Histórico del Cuzco*, II (1951), 225–269.

In his gloss on Ley II, Título XXIII, Segunda Partida of the *Siete Partidas*, which was entitled "Por que razones se mueven los omes a fazer guerra", López quotes Cayetan, the great commentator on Aquinas, that "no es justo pretender que se haga la guerra para extender el Evangelio, porque Jesús envió sus discípulos en misión fraterna y de paz, no como guerreros, y nadie puede ser llamado a la fuerza para recibir la fe". López was one of the jurists of the age who had much experience in affairs of the Indies, and his work merits investigation.

4. Narciso Alonso Cortés, "Fray Bartolomé de Las Casas en Valladolid", *Revista de Indias*, I (Madrid, 1940), 105–111.

5. Detailed information on these treatises and their translations will be found in *Las Casas. Bibliografía crítica*, pp. 139–156. One modern writer feels that the Las Casas-Sepúlveda dispute helps to explain, along with the restrictions on foreigners going to the Indies, why the Indies did not attract many non-Iberian missionaries. Lázaro de Aspurz, "La

idea misional fuera de la Península Ibérica en los siglos XVI y XVII", *Missionalia Hispanica*, I (Madrid, 1944), 504.

6. "Las Casas y el movimiento indigenista en España y América en la primera mitad del siglo XIV", *Revista de Historia de América* (1952), no. 34, pp. 339–411; "Don Juan del Valle, primer obispo de Popayán", *Estudios Segovianos*, IV (1952), 39–58.

7. Ignacio Bejarano, ed., *Actas de cabildo de la ciudad de México* (7 vols., Mexico, 1889–1900), VI, 128.

8. Losada, *Sepúlveda a través de su "Epistolario"*, p. 154.

9. José Toribio Medina, *Biblioteca hispano-americana* (7 vols., Santiago de Chile, 1898–1907), I, 261.

10. Fabié, *Vida y escritos de Las Casas*, II, 545–549.

11. The poem was written by Luis Hurtado de Toledo and Micael de Caravajal and is printed in *Biblioteca de Autores Españoles*, XXV, 1–41. A recent interpretation, which sees in the poem a reflection of the Valladolid dispute, is by Juan A. Ortega y Medina, "El indio absuelto y las Indias condenadas en las Cortes de la Muerte", *Historia Mexicana*, IV (Abril-Junio, 1955), 477–505. This interpretation has not been clearly established, in my opinion. The attitude of Ortega y Medina towards the 1550 controversy itself may be seen from his description of the application of Aristotle's theory: "como lo argumentaba pía y cristianísimamente el tomista Dr. Sepúlveda" (p. 498). The poem did show, however, that the author knew and used the *Brevísima Relación* of Las Casas, as Morínigo points out, *América en el teatro de Lope de Vega*, pp. 42–47.

12. Marcel Bataillon, "Vasco de Quiroga et Bartolomé de Las Casas", *Revista de Historia de América* (1952), no. 33, pp. 83–95.

13. José M. Gallegos Rocafull, *El pensamiento mexicano en los siglos XVI y XVII* (Mexico, 1951), p. 192. The "Información" is printed in *Documentos inéditos de América*, X, 333–513.

14. *Documentos inéditos de América*, X, 351.

15. *Ibid.*, pp. 346–348, 354, 377–379, 383–384, 471, 484.

16. *Ibid.*, p. 354.

17. Rafael Aguayo Spencer, ed., *Don Vasco de Quiroga-Documentos* (Mexico, 1939), pp. 84, 216. The principal document referred to is Juan José Moreno, *Fragmentos de la vida y virtudes del Illmo. . . . Vasco de Quiroga . . .* (Mexico, 1766).

18. Printed in *Cuerpo de documentos del siglo XVI sobre los derechos de España en las Indias y las Filipinas*, Agustín Millares Carlo and Lewis Hanke, eds. (Mexico, 1943), pp. 3–9.

19. Fabié, *Vida y escritos de Las Casas*, II, 302.

20. Medina, *Biblioteca hispano-americana*, I, 369–378.

21. *Biblioteca de Autores Españoles*, LXV, 232–233.

22. On this little-known figure see the volume edited by Millares Carlo and the writer, *Cuerpo de documentos del siglo XVI*, pp. xix–xxiii. The Yugoslavian Dominican Rev. Antoninus Zaninović of Dubrovnik writes in a recent letter that he is preparing a study on this relatively unknown Dalmatian.

23. Alonso de Zorita, *Historia de la Nueva España* (Madrid, 1909), p. ii.

24. Juan de Solórzano Pereira, *De jure Indiarum* (Madrid, 1629), Libro II, cap. 1, no. 33.

25. Vicente Beltrán de Heredia, O.P., *El maestro Juan de la Peña*, O.P. (Salamanca, 1935), p. 79.

26. Fabié, *Vida y escritos de Las Casas*, II, 550–566.

27. Quoted by Bataillon, *Erasmo en España*, II, 237.

28. *Controversias ilustres . . .* , edited by Fidel Rodríguez Alcalde (Valladolid, 1931), pp. 8–10.

29. *Actas de cabildo de México*, VI, 316–317, 358, 383, 442; VII, 30, 74.

30. *Crónica de la Nueva España* (Madrid, 1914), Chap. 16. The quotation comes from p. 32.

31. *Actas de cabildo de México*, VI, 492–493.

32. Antonine Tibesar, ed., "Instructions for the confessors of conquistadores issued by the Archbishop of Lima in 1560", *The Americas*, III (Washington, D.C., 1947), 514–534.

33. The text of this order is in Richard Konetzke, ed., *Colección de documentos para la historia de la formación social de Hispanoamérica, 1493–1810* (Madrid, 1951?), pp. 335–339.

34. *Itinerario para parrochos de indios* (Antwerp, 1774), Libro II, trat. 9, sec. 15.

35. *Documentos inéditos del siglo XVI para la historia de México*, edited by Mariano Cuevas (Mexico, 1914), pp. 322–323.

36. Archivo de Indias, Charcas 16.

37. By the writer in *Spanish Struggle for Justice*, pp. 133–146.

38. Joaquín García Icazbalceta, *Colección de documentos para la historia de México* (2 vols., Mexico, 1866), II, 511–512.

39. On Paul III's difficulties with Charles V, see the writer's *Pope Paul III and the American Indians*. One of the certain ways to rouse royal anger was to appeal to the pope, and the Franciscan Motolinía insinuated in his fiery 1555 letter to Charles V that Las Casas "might go to Rome and there cause difficulties at the papal court", *Documentos inéditos de América*, VII, 267.

40. García Icazbalceta, *Colección de documentos para la historia de México*, II, 599–600. Las Casas apparently never tried to get the Council of Trent to support his views. Bishops in America were excused from attending the council as new world problems were not emphasized,

Francisco Mateos, S.J., "Ecos de América en Trento", *Revista de Indias*, año VI, no. 22 (Madrid, 1945), 559–605. Additional material on papal attempts; immediately after the close of the Council of Trent in 1563, to get more power in American affairs may be found in Pedro de Leturia, "Felipe II y el pontificado en un momento culminante de la historia hispanoamericana", *Estudios Eclesiásticos*, número extraordinario (Madrid, 1928); Robert Charles Padden, "The Ordenanza del Patronazgo, 1574: An Interpretative Essay", *The Americas* (Washington, D.C., 1956), 333–354; and in the *Indices de la correspondencia entre la nunciatura en España y la Santa Sede, durante el reinado de Felipe II*, edited by José Olarra Garmendia and María Luisa Larramendi (2 vols., Madrid, 1948–1949).

The information on Las Casas and the papacy presented here comes largely from an unpublished note on "Última gestión del P. Las Casas en favor de los indios" by Manuel María Martínez, O.P., of Madrid, who was kind enough to permit me to use it.

41. *Historiadores de Indias*, edited by Manuel Serrano y Sanz (2 vols., Madrid, 1909), II, 562.

42. Pedro de Quiroga, *Libro intitulado Coloquios de la verdad*, edited by Julián Zarco Cuevas (Seville, 1922), p. 17.

43. Many examples could be provided. The present one comes from Howard F. Cline, "Civil Congregation of the Western Chinantec, New Spain, 1599–1603", *The Americas*, XII (Washington, D.C., 1955), 133.

44. As may be seen, for example, in Manuel da Nóbrega, *Diálogo sobre a conversão de gentio*, edited by Serafím Leite, S.J. (Lisbon, 1954).

45. D'Olwer, *Fray Bernardino de Sahagún*, p. 151; Villoro, *Los grandes momentos del indigenismo en Mexico*, p. 39.

46. Villoro, *Los grandes momentos del indigenismo en Mexico*, p. 68.

47. D'Olwer, *Fray Bernardino de Sahagún*, p. 173.

48. The writer has studied these instructions in "The Development of Regulations for Conquistadores", *Contribuciones para el estudio de la historia de América. Homenaje al doctor Emilio Ravignani* (Buenos Aires, 1941), pp. 12–15.

49. Manzano, *La incorporación de las Indias*, pp. 151–217, devotes much attention to the Valladolid dispute. The reference to Ovando appears on pp. 203–206. José de la Peña y Cámara, Director of the Archivo de Indias, has in preparation a work on the contributions of Ovando to the administration of the Indies.

50. Manzano, *La incorporación de las Indias*, p. 210. A later summary of Manzano's views may be found in his volume *La adquisición de las Indias por los Reyes Católicos y su incorporación a los reinos castellanos* (Madrid, 1951).

51. The text of the 1573 ordinance may be conveniently found in *Documentos inéditos de América*, XVI, 142–187.

52. José Miranda, *El tributo indígena en la Nueva España durante el siglo XVI* (Mexico, 1952), p. 147.

53. John H. Rowe, "The Incas under Spanish Colonial Institutions", *Hispanic American Historical Review*, XXXVII (1957), 155–199.

54. *Documentos inéditos de América*, XVI, 152. For a detailed explanation of the special religious and political significance of the term *Pacificación* in Spanish legislation for the Indies, see Rafael Altamira, *Diccionario castellano de palabras jurídicas y técnicas tomadas de la legislación indiana*, pp. 228–230. Questions of terminology still agitate historians and governments. A campaign is being carried on, initiated by the Argentine Ricardo Levene, to see that Spanish territory in America be referred to as "Kingdoms" and never as "Colonies". See his volume *Las Indias no eran colonias* (Buenos Aires, 1951). The Portuguese have also recently manifested a concern for such matters. The word *império* is now proscribed, as is *colónia*; the officially approved terms are *Ultramar* and *Províncias Ultramarinas*.

55. Sverker Arnoldsson remarks on this polarization in his *Los momentos históricos de América* (Madrid, 1956), pp. 35–36.

56. López described his military exploits in a letter to his provincial dated June 11, 1576. Francisco Mateos, S.J., "Primeros pasos en la envangelización de los indios (1568–1576)", *Missionalia Hispanica*, IV (Madrid, 1947), 43. The seventeenth-century jurist Juan de Solórzano Pereira also stated that he believed war sometimes necessary, on the basis of his experience in Peru, Antonio de Egaña, S.J., "La función misionera del poder civil, según Juan de Solórzano Pereira (1575–1655)", *Studia Missionalia*, VI (Rome, 1951), 91–92. For material on Sánchez, see my *Cuerpo de documentos*, pp. xliii–xliv. For additional information, see Francisco Colin, *Labor evangélica*... (3 vols., edited by Pablo Pastells, Barcelona, 1900–1902).

57. His basic writings have recently been edited, with an introduction by Francisco Mateos, S.J., *Obras del P. José de Acosta* (Madrid, 1954).

58. *Ibid.*, pp. 394–396.

59. *Ibid.*, pp. 396–399.

60. *Ibid.*, p. 397.

61. *Ibid.*, pp. 507–508.

62. *Ibid.*, pp. 435–437. For a substantial treatment of Acosta's juridical thought, see Antonio Gómez Robledo, "Las ideas jurídicas del P. José de Acosta", *Revista de la Escuela Nacional de Jurisprudencia*, II, nos. 7–8 (Mexico, 1940), 297–313.

63. *Obras del P. José de Acosta*, pp. 437–438. For a confirmation of

this interpretation, and for some other interesting material, see Antonio de Egaña, S.J., "El P. Diego de Avendaño, S.J. (1594–1688) y la tesis teocrática 'Papa, Dominus Orbis'", *Archivum Historicum Societatis Jesu*, XVIII (1949), 212.

64. *Obras del P. José de Acosta*, p. xv. The contradictory views of the early Jesuits in Peru are given by Antonio de Egaña, S.J., "La visión humanística del indio americano en los primeros jesuítas peruanos", *Analecta Gregoriana*, LXX (Rome, 1954), 291–306.

65. *Obras del P. José de Acosta*, p. 477. "Jesús mío, qué desorden, cuánta fealdad!" are the words he uses.

66. *Ibid.* "De los soberbios templos de Méjico" (pp. 153–155); "De la confesión y confesores que usaban los indios" (pp. 168–170); "De otras ceremonias y ritos de los indios, a semejanza de los nuestros" (pp. 173–174); "Que es falsa la opinión de los que tienen los indios por hombres faltos de entendimiento" (pp. 182–183); "Del modo de cómputo y calendario que usaban los mejicanos" (pp. 183–184). Many other pertinent chapters on Indian culture are to be found in Libros V–VII.

67. *Ibid.*, pp. 492–500.

68. *Ibid.*, p. 450.

69. *Ibid.*, p. 182.

70. *Ibid.*, pp. 182–183.

71. Phelan, *The Millennial Kingdom of the Franciscans in the New World*, pp. 62–63. Phelan also points out that Dante and Sepúlveda held closely similar views on race questions and on imperialism.

72. Juan de Silva, *Advertencias importantes acerca del buen gobierno y administración de las Indias assi en lo espiritual como en lo temporal* (Madrid, 1621), f. 12. A copy is in the British Museum. Earlier in 1613, Silva had submitted two printed memorials which have the same tenor as his later statement. (British Museum. Additional MS. 13,977. Folios 203–235.) Fr. Pedro de Zevallos and half a dozen other Franciscans supported strongly Silva's doctrine. (British Museum. 521. 1. F. (1). Folios 1–6.)

73. Eduardo Arcila Farías, *La doctrina de la justa guerra contra los indios en Venezuela* (Caracas, 1954). Some of the later applications of the peaceful preaching doctrine have been collected by the writer in the introduction to the Las Casas treatise *Del único modo de atraer a todos los pueblos a la verdadera religión*, edited by Agustín Millares Carlo (Mexico, 1942), pp. xxxix–xlii. On the successful pacification policy used along the northern frontier of New Spain at the close of the sixteenth century, after "guerra a fuego y a sangre" had failed, see Philip W. Powell, *Soldiers Indians and Silver* (Berkeley and Los Angeles, 1952), pp. 181–223.

74. *Las Casas. Bibliografía crítica*, pp. 213–214. His rare works are in the British Museum. The reference to his use of the Valladolid dispute material is to be found in *Controversias antiguas de la misión de la China* (1679), fol. 426. Another example of the way the basic issues discussed by Las Casas and Sepúlveda later appeared in other quarters may be seen from the lively controversy over the nature of the Philippine natives as recorded in Juan J. Delgado's *Historia General sacro-profana, política y natural de las islas del poniente llamadas Filipinas* (Manila, 1892), tomo único, chaps. VI–VII–VIII. In the course of his refutation of the remarks by Fray Gaspar de Agustín against the Filipinos, Delgado pointed out that in Asia "the heathen seldom oppose our preaching, and if they do oppose, it is not because they disbelieve it, nor out of zeal for their own rites, but for motives which are purely temporal and political: either because they fear that they will be subjugated by the Spaniards, or that they will be made to pay an onerous tribute, or that they may be enslaved or killed. And thus experience has taught us that when the missionaries have ventured among them entirely deprived of temporal support, and only armed with zeal for God's honour, they have made more fruit than in those regions where they have been protected by the King's weapons. And what is more, the only missions which have achieved permanence and stability are those where the missionaries have delivered themselves into the hands of the heathen, trusting in divine help."

Two recent works on the early years of the conquest in the Philippines are Jesús Gayo Aragón, *Ideas jurídico-teológicas de los religiosos de Filipinas en el siglo XVI sobre la conquista de las islas* (Manila, 1950); and John Leddy Phelan, "Some Ideological Aspects of the Conquest of the Philippines", *The Americas*, XIII (Washington, D.C., 1957), no. 3, pp. 221–239.

75. Cited by Friede, *Las Casas y el movimiento indigenista*, p. 348.

76. Cited by Manuel Giménez Fernández, *Bartolomé de Las Casas. Volumen Primero. Delegado de Cisneros para la reformación de las Indias (1516–1517)* (Seville, 1953), p. 152. Sigüenza described the Indians as "aquella bárbara y miserable gente propios hijos de maldito Chanaan, nacidos al parecer para esclavos miserables de sus hermanos como lo profetizó el gran Padre Noé".

77. Ricardo Levene, *En el tercer centenario de "Política Indiana" de Juan de Solórzano Pereira* (Buenos Aires, 1948), p. 39.

78. Solórzano, *Política indiana*, Lib. I, cap. IX, nos. 20–36.

79. See José de Onís, ed., "The letter of Francisco Iturri, S.J. (1789). Its importance for Hispanic-American history", *The Americas*, VIII (Washington, D.C., 1951), no. 1, pp. 85–90; and above all Gerbi. *Viejas polémicas sobre el nuevo mundo*, chaps. 3–5. Gerbi has just published

another solid work as a continuation, *La disputa del Nuovo Mundo: Storia di una polemica, 1750–1900*.

80. Silvio Zavala and José Miranda, "Instituciones indígenas en la colonia", *Memorias del Instituto Nacional Indigenista*, VI (Mexico, 1954), 103.

81. Ricard, *Conquista spiritual de México*, p. 419.

82. *Las Casas. Bibliografía crítica*, pp. 253–254, 256, 263–265, 338–339, 355. The repercussion of Gregoire's ideas in Argentina has been studied by Roberto I. Peña, *Vitoria y Sepúlveda y el problema del indio en la antigua gobernación de Tucumán* (Córdoba, Argentina, 1951).

83. *Cartas mejicanas escritas por d. Benito María de Moxó y de Francoli año de 1805* (second edition, Genoa, n.d.), p. 207.

84. *Viejas polémicas sobre el nuevo mundo*, p. 65.

85. James F. King, "The Colored Castes and American Representation in the Cortes of Cádiz", *Hispanic American Historical Review*, XXXIII (1953), 43.

86. *Las Casas. Bibliografía crítica*, p. 256.

87. See his preface to Sepúlveda's treatise, *Boletín de la Real Academia de la Historia*, XXI (Madrid, 1892), 257–369. See also *Las Casas. Bibliografía crítica*, p. 282–285.

Of course Positivists were not uniformly in favour of the "survival of the fittest" creed. In Brazil, for example, Positivists led in the movement to protect the Indians. See the doctoral dissertation by David H. Stauffer at the University of Texas, "The Origin and Establishment of Brazil's Indian Service: 1889–1910" (Austin, 1955).

88. *Las Casas. Bibliografía crítica*, pp. 279–280.

89. *Ibid.*, pp. 335, 394. Oswald Robles has this to say: "La voz de Las Casas, en la controversia con Sepúlveda solamente anunciaba, con pequeñas inconsecuencias lógicas, la incomovible tesis de la escuela de Salamanca", *Filósofos mexicanos del siglo XVI* (Mexico, 1950), pp. 122–123.

90. Juan Comas, "Los detractores del protector universal de indios y la realidad histórica", *Miscelánea de estudios dedicados a Fernando Ortiz*, (3 vols., La Habana, 1955–1957), I, 369–393.

91. Edmundo O'Gorman, "Sobre la naturaleza bestial del indio americano", *Filosofía y Letras* (Mexico, 1941), no. 3, p. 145; Gunther Krauss, "La duda victoriana ante la conquista de América", *Arbor*, XII (Madrid, 1952), 353; J. H. Parry, *English Historical Review*, LXVII (July, 1952), 408; Bell, *Juan Ginés de Sepúlveda*, p. 38; Roberto Levillier, *Don Francisco de Toledo, supremo organizador del Perú; su vida, su obra (1515–1582)* (2 vols., Buenos Aires, 1935), I, 177. It is instructive to note that in one of the most recent—and most sophisticated, witty, and tendentious—defences of Spain's work in America, the name of Sepúlveda

and his doctrine of natural slavery do not appear, Francisco Morales Padrón, *Historia negativa de España en América* (Madrid, 1956).

92. Rafael Arévalo Martínez, "De Aristóteles a Hitler", *Boletín de la Biblioteca Nacional* (Guatemala, 1945), tercera época, no. 1, pp. 3–4.

93. Venancio D. Carro, *La ciencia tomista*, LXXIX (Salamanca, 1952), 122–124.

94. In the introduction to the facsimile reproduction of the *Recopilación de leyes de los reynos de las Indias* (3 vols., Madrid, 1943).

CHAPTER VIII

1. Ángel Losada, "*Los tesoros del Perú* y *La apología contra Sepúlveda,* obras inéditas de Fr. Bartolomé de las Casas", *Boletín de la Real Academia de la Historia*, CXXXI (Madrid, 1953), 332. Losada bases his supposition on a statement made in 1636 by the historian Antonio Fuertes y Viota. Charles V was undoubtedly busy, as may easily be seen from Bohdan Chudoba, *Spain and the Empire, 1519–1643* (Chicago, 1952).

2. *Supra*, pp. 86–88.

3. Las Casas, *Colección de tratados*, pp. 136–137. On Soto generally see Carro, *Domingo de Soto y su doctrina jurídica.*

4. *Politics*, Book VII, Ch. 7.

5. W. W. Tarn, *Alexander the Great and the Unity of Mankind* (London, 1933), p. 7. See also pp. 3, 21, 28. Originally published in *Proceedings of the British Academy*, XIX. Recent research seems to indicate that a variety of explanations may be offered for Alexander's ideas, but it also appears that most students accept the fact that he held the ideas on the fusion of races attributed to him, C. A. Robinson, Jr., "The Extraordinary Ideas of Alexander the Great", *American Historical Review*, LXII (1957), 326–344. For a fuller explanation of the view that "Alexander was the first man known to us who contemplated the brotherhood of man or the unity of mankind", see Robinson's essay on "Alexander the Great and the Barbarians", in *Classical Studies Presented to Edward Capps* (Princeton, 1936), 298–305.

6. Paul Gaffarel, *Histoire du Brésil Français au Seizième Siècle* (Paris, 1878), pp. 239–262.

7. *The Cosmographical Glasse* (London, 1559), fols. 200–201.

8. Wesley Frank Craven, "Indian Policy in Early Virginia", *William and Mary Quarterly*, I (1944), 72–73.

9. Louis B. Wright, *Religion and Empire* (Chapel Hill, 1943), p. 86.

10. Garrett Mattingly, *Renaissance Diplomacy* (Boston, 1955), p. 290.

11. *The History of Carolina* (Charlotte, North Carolina, 1903), p. 141.

12. Archdale, "A New Description of that Fertile and Pleasant Province of Carolina . . . (1707)", in B. R. Carroll, *Historical Collections of South Carolina*, II (2 vols., New York, 1836), 88–89.

13. Margaret T. Hodgen, "The Doctrine of Survivals: the History of an Idea", *American Anthropologist*, new series, XXX (1931), 307–324.

14. E. B. Reuter, ed., *Race and Culture of the South Seas* (Sydney, Australia, 1935), p. 171.

15. Thomas Dunbabin, *Slaves of the South Seas* (Sydney, Australia, 1935), p. 171.

16. James Bonwick, *The Last of the Tasmanians* (London, 1870), p. 324.

17. D. J. Cunningham, "Anthropology in the Eighteenth Century", *Journal of the Royal Anthropological Institute*, XXXVIII (London, 1908), 12.

18. T. Wingate Todd, "An Anthropologist's Study of Negro Life", *Journal of Negro History*, XVI (1931), 36.

19. *Incidents of Travel in Central America, Chiapas, and Yucatan*, edited by Richard L. Predmore (2 vols., New Brunswick, New Jersey, 1949), I, 80–81.

20. Felix von Luschan, "Anthropological View of Race", in *Papers on Inter-Racial Problems*, edited by G. Spiller (London, 1911), pp. 15–16. Margaret T. Hodgen, *The Doctrine of Survivals* (London, 1936), pp. 20–21. Much information may also be found in William S. Jenkins, *Pro-Slavery Thought in the Old South* (Chapel Hill, North Carolina, 1935).

21. See the essay by the Bolivian historian Humberto Vázquez-Machicado, "La sociología de René-Moreno", in his *Tres ensayos históricos* (La Paz, 1937), pp. 85–110.

22. Kenneth M. Stampp, "The Historian and Southern Negro Slavery", *American Historical Review*, LVII (1952), 613. A full scale description of the influence of mythology on both practical men and scholars is Melville J. Herskovits, *The Myth of the Negro Past* (New York, 1941). See particularly the conclusions on pp. 292–300. Other material on race and race mixture may be found in the writer's article, "Gilberto Freyre: Brazilian Social Historian", *The Quarterly Journal of Inter-American Relations*, I (Cambridge—Mass., 1939), 24–44.

23. Hans Kohn, *Nationalism. Its Meaning and History* (Princeton, 1955), p. 180.

24. An excellent series of articles on the theory and practice of *Apartheid* ran in the *Manchester Guardian Weekly* for April 1, April 29, May 6, 1954.

25. New York, 1954.

26. New York, 1954. It is necessary to refer to such books because of

the unctuous self-satisfaction with which some non-Spaniards view Spain. An English pamphlet of about 1707 entitled *Proposals Concerning the Propagating of Christian Knowledge in the Highlands and Islands of Scotland and Forraign Parts of the World* has this to say: "But it may be justly believed that Popery is not Christianity, so some of their own Writers have confessed, that the Christian Religion hath not been by them duely Preached in the Indies: And it is well known that Barthal Casas a Bishop of their own, complaineth that the unheard of Cruelties and Covetousness of the Spaniards bred woeful prejudice, both against the Christians God and their Religion in the West-Indies." This rare item was listed in Catalogue No. 754 of Francis Edwards Ltd., *The American Continent* (London, 1955), p. 53.

27. G. H. Calpin, ed., *The South African Way of Life. Values and Ideals of a Multi-Racial Society* (New York, 1954), p. 55.

28. *Ibid.*, pp. 48–69, in a chapter by a Bantu named Selby Bangani Ngcobo entitled "The Bantu Peoples". Perhaps some day a general law will be worked out to demonstrate that under certain conditions a feeling of superiority develops in all peoples. An unpublished study by Hortense Powdermaker found "that African children at a secondary school were unanimous that Africans were superior to Europeans in generosity, kindliness, and hospitality". Philip Mason, *Christianity and Race* (London, 1956), p. 14. Attitudes may, however, be modified. Mason also refers to a Protestant missionary, David Lindley, who "after nearly forty years in Africa wrote home to his society in America that he had begun to suspect there was after all some virtue in the *lobola* of the Zulus. This he had at first regarded as the price of a bride and condemned it entirely. . . ." He came to see that, as it worked in practice, *lobola* gave a number of the wife's relations a material interest in the continuance of the marriage and thus "performed a useful social function", *ibid.*, pp. 146–147. The Spaniards and Negroes in Cuba have generally considered the Chinese immigrants who went there in the nineteenth century as their social and intellectual inferiors, Duvon C. Corbitt, "Chinese Immigrants in Cuba", *Far Eastern Survey*, XIII, no. 14 (New York, July 12, 1944), pp. 130–132. See also Corbitt's *Chinese in Cuba* (New York, 1944), especially Chap. VI on "Coolie Life in Cuba".

29. "Must we Rewrite the History of Imperialism?", *Historical Studies. Australia and New Zealand* (Melbourne, November, 1953), VI, no. 21, pp. 90–98.

30. *Moral Man and Immoral Society* (New York, 1948), p. 8.

31. Friede, *Las Casas y el movimiento indigenista*, p. 353.

32. Orwell in 1946 had this to say in his *A Collection of Essays* (1954), p. 173: "In our time, political speech and writing are largely the defence

154   NOTES: CHAPTER VIII

of the indefensible. . . . Defenceless villages are bombarded from the
air, the inhabitants driven out into the countryside, the cattle machine-
gunned, the huts set on fire with incendiary bullets: this is called
pacification."

33. Antonine Tibesar, "The Alternativa: A Study in Spanish-Creole
Relations in Seventeenth-Century Peru", *The Americas*, XI (1953),
no. 3, pp. 230–231.

34. Moisés Sáenz, *Sobre el indio peruano y su incorporación al medio
nacional* (Mexico, 1933), p. 168.

35. Luis Monguió, *La poesía postmodernista peruana* (Berkeley and
Los Angeles, 1955), p. 105.

36. "Debates sobre temas sociológicos. Relaciones interamericanas",
Sur (Buenos Aires, Sept., 1940), no. 72, pp. 100–123. This article is a
report of a round-table discussion, in which various writers of the
Americas participated. The quotation comes from some remarks by
Arnaldo Orfila Reynal, which appeared on p. 114.

37. *Ibid.*

38. Buenos Aires, 1952, pp. 32, 172–173, 319.

39. Venancio D. Carro, "Bartolomé de Las Casas y las controversias
teológico jurídicas de Indias", *Boletín de la Real Academia de la Historia*,
CXXXI (Madrid, 1953), 260.

40. Diego Clemencín, "De la poca lenidad de los eclesiásticos en el
siglo de la Reina Católica. Máximas de inhumanidad e injusticia
respecto de los moros en aquel tiempo", *Memorias de la Real Academia
de la Historia*, VI (1821), 389–395. Other pertinent material is to be
found in P. Boronat y Barrachina, *Los moriscos españoles y su expulsión*
(2 vols., Valencia, 1901). Robert Ricard has written some suggestive
studies on the relationship between Moors and Indians: "Indiens et
Morisques", *Etudes et documents pour l'histoire missionaire de l'Espagne et
du Portugal* (Louvain, 1931), pp. 209–219; "Granada y América",
*Primer centenario de la Sociedad Mexicana de Geografía y Estadística, 1833–
1933* (2 vols., Mexico, 1933), I, 245–247. See also Marcos Jiménez de la
Espada, "La guerra del moro a fines del siglo XV", *Boletín de la Real
Academia de la Historia*, XXV (Madrid, 1894), 170–212. Slaves were
obtained in Valencia in 1483 by "Just war", Leopoldo Piles, "Situación
social de los moros en Valencia, siglo XV", *Estudios de historia social de
España*, I (Madrid, 1949), 225–274. In 1485 Ferdinand reported on the
conquest of towns near Granada that "destos que se tomaron por fuerça
slauas las mujeres e ninyos, todos los barones se pusieron al espada".
Richard Konetzke, "La esclavitud de los indios como elemento en la
estructuración social de Hispanoamérica", *ibid.*, p. 446. Balboa even
advocated the extirpation of Indians by burning them, because they
were "tan mala gente" (*ibid.*, p. 446), but the Crown soon came to

distinguish between wars against the Moors and those against Indians. Elies Serra i Ràfols shows, however, what might have happened in the Indies had the Spanish conscience not been aroused on behalf of the Indians; in the Canary Islands in 1489 the Catholic Kings agreed to the slavery of certain Canarians on account of their supposed heresy, although in fact they were Christians. "Els Reis Catòlics i l'esclavitud", *Revista de Catalunya*, Any 5 (Barcelona, 1928), 368–378.

It should also be remembered that papal precedents existed. The bull *Dum diversas* of Nicholas V sent on June 18, 1452, to Alfonso V conceded him general authorization "d'attaquer, conquérir et soumettre les sarrasins, païens et autres infidèles ennemis du Christ: de s'emparer de leurs territoires et de leurs biens; de soumettre leur personne en perpetuelle servitude et de transmettre territoires et biens à ses successeurs". Ch.-M. de Witte, "Les bulles pontificales et l'expansion portugaise au XVᵉ siècle", *Revue d'Histoire Ecclésiastique*, L (1950), 425.

41. R. de Lafuente Machaín, *Los portugueses en Buenos Aires. Siglo XVII* (Madrid, 1931), p. 31.

42. João de Barros, *Asia*, First Decade, Book V, Chap. 1. A recent study is Margarida Barradas de Carvalho, "L'idéologie religieuse dans la 'Crónica dos feitos de Guiné' de Gomes Eanes de Zurara", *Bulletin des Etudes Portugaises*, XIX (Lisbon, 1956), 5–34. There has also been discovered in the Torre do Tombo a manuscript entitled "Porq̃ causas see pode mouer guerra justa cõtra infieles". Dated about 1550, it develops an argument similar to the doctrine of Las Casas against Sepúlveda. See Costa Brochado, "A espiritualidade dos descobrimentos e conquistas dos portugueses", *Portugal em Africa*, segunda serie, III (Lisbon, 1946), 232–240. The text of the treatise appears on pp. 235–240.

Other Portuguese shared the ideas of Sepúlveda. According to one sixteenth-century document, "muitos se dirigem a India para defender e propagar a fé católica, quer pela pregação do Evangelho quer pela força das armas". Domingos Mauricio Gomes dos Santos, S.J., "A missa a bordo das naus da India", *Las Ciencias*, año XVII, no. 4 (Madrid), p. 738. Finally, W. G. L. Randles has well advanced a dissertation on "South-East Africa in the European Mind in the Sixteenth Century".

43. Some information on Portuguese missionary activity is provided by George C. A. Boehrer, "The Franciscans and Portuguese Colonization in Africa and the Atlantic Islands, 1415–1499", *The Americas*, XI (Washington, D.C., 1955), no. 3, pp. 389–404.

44. Welch, *Europe's Discovery of South Africa*, p. 321.

45. On struggles in Brazil against Indian slavery see J. M. de Madureira, "A liberdade dos indios e a companhia de Jesus", *Revista*

do Instituto Histórico e Geográphico Brasileiro. Tomo especial, Congresso Internacional de Historia de America, IV (1927), 1–160; and Mathias C. Kieman, *The Indian Policy of Portugal in the Amazon Region, 1614–1693* (Washington, D.C., 1954).

46. Robert Southey, *History of Brazil* (London, 1810), I, 259. Despite this and other similar occurrences, some Brazilians have prided themselves on the treatment given their Indians in comparison with those in Spanish America. See Norberto J. A. Jorge, "A catechese e civilisação dos indios no Brasil", *Annaes do Primeiro Congresso Brasileiro de Geographia na cidade do Rio de Janeiro de 7 a 16 de setembro de 1909* (Rio de Janeiro, 1911), pp. 206–208. Dr. David H. Stauffer was kind enough to give me this last reference, in which the *Brevíssima Relación* of Las Casas was cited to show that Spaniards were more cruel than Portuguese to American Indians.

The seventeenth-century Portuguese authority on international law, Serafim de Freitas, in *De Justo Imperio Lusitanorum Asiatico* boasted that no people had been subjugated by Portuguese kings under the pretext of religion. Welch, *Europe's Discovery of South Africa*, p. 140.

The nineteenth-century Brazilian historian Francisco Adolfo de Varnhagen had this to say about Las Casas and his peaceful preaching ideas:

"As providencias de mal entendida filantropia, decretadas depois pela piedade dos reis, e sustentadas pela política dos jesuitas, foram a causa de que os índios começassem pouco a pouco a ser únicamente chamadas à civilização pelos demourados meios da catequese, e que ainda restem tantos nos sertões, devorandose uns aos outros, vexando o país e degradando a humanidade. Era uma verdadeira monomania do pseudo-filantrópico Las Casas a de deixar aos Americanos todos no mesmo estado em que estavam", *Historia geral do Brasil*, fifth edition (edited by Rodolfo Garcia, 5 vols., São Paulo, n.d.), Tomo 1, Sec. XIII, p. 259.

47. Felipe Barreda Laos considered the Valladolid dispute an important part of the intellectual history of Peru, minutely described the theories involved, and pointed out that Domingo de Santo Tomás and many others in the colleges and universities supported Las Casas. *Vida intelectual del virreinato del Perú* (Buenos Aires, 1937), pp. 65–97, 371–372.

48. "Discurso sobre Fray Bartolomé de Las Casas", *Boletín del Archivo Nacional*, XLI (Havana, 1942), 106.

49. Rafael Altamira, "Resultados generales en el estudio de la historia colonial americana. Criterio histórico resultante", *XXI Congreso Internacional de americanistas* (La Haya, 1924), p. 431. See also Carro, *Bartolomé de Las Casas y las controversias de Indias*, p. 267.

50. Altamira, *A History of Spain*, trans. by Muna Lee (New York, 1949), p. 358.

51. Archivo de Indias, Filipinas 339, Libro DDI, Parte II, f. 155 vuelto. Problems on baptism also developed in the Philippines, John Leddy Phelan, "Pre-baptismal instruction and the Administration of Baptism in the Philippines during the Sixteenth Century", *The Americas*, XII (Washington, D.C., 1955), no. 1, pp. 3–23.

52. *Recopilación de leyes de los reinos de las Indias*, Libro III, título 4, ley 9.

53. The Colombian Juan Friede urges this view, pointing out that Las Casas was largely supported by the Crown and by an important segment of society, "Fray Bartolomé de Las Casas, exponente del movimiento indigenista del siglo XVI", *Revista de Indias*, año XIII (Madrid, 1953), 25–55. A Spaniard has also advocated this approach, Luciano Pereña Vicente, *La Universidad de Salamanca, forja del pensamiento político español en el siglo XVI* (Salamanca, 1954).

54. Information supplied by Professor Pedro Sáinz Rodríguez, of Lisbon.

55. Information supplied by Professor Manuel Giménez Fernández, of Seville. Las Casas held passionate convictions on many subjects, and this has sometimes led to his being attacked on extraneous issues quite remote from his main ideas. He felt strongly, for example, that Columbus was robbed by Amerigo Vespucci of the honour of having the New World named after him. As a reaction to this Germán Arciniegas, the latest biographer of Vespucci, intent on proving that *his* hero has in turn been maligned, belittles Las Casas as a thinker and points the finger of scorn at him as a believer in magic. See *Amerigo and the New World* (New York, 1955), pp. 303–305, for the latest manifestation of the heat generated. One is reminded of the declaration of one sixteenth-century friar, in trying to explain the endless controversy over the nature of the Indians: "Esta de verdad es materia en la qual un abismo llama otro abismo ... todas las cosas de aquestos indios son un abismo de confusion lleno de mil cataractas, del qual salen mil confusiones e inconvenientes ... y no ay cosa que para ellos se ordene que no salgan della mil inconvenientes. De tal manera que aunque lo que se ordena sea en si bueno y con sancta intencion provehido, quando se viene a aplicar a la subjeta materia sale dañoso y desordenado y redunda en daño y disminucion de aquellos a quien bien queremos hazer." Friar Domingo de Betanzos in an undated letter to the Council of the Indies, *Archivo Histórico Nacional* (Madrid), Cartas de Indias, Caja 2, Num. 124.

56. Las Casas, *Apologética historia*, pp. 127–128.

57. See his *Instructions for Governing the Interior Provinces of New Spain, 1786*, edited by Donald Worcester (Berkeley, 1951), p. 43.

58. Roger J. Williams, *Free and Unequal. The Biological Basis of Individual Liberty* (Austin, Texas, 1953). Another book of general value is Henry Alonzo Myers, *Are Men Equal? An Enquiry into the Meaning of American Democracy* (Ithaca, 1955).

59. Las Casas, *Historia de las Indias*, I, prólogo.

60. The phrase "auténtica furia española" comes from José M. Gallegos Rocafull, *El hombre y el mundo de los teólogos españoles de los siglos de oro* (Mexico, 1946), p. 14.

Alain Guy, *Esquisse des progrès de la spéculation philosophique et théologique à Salamanque au cours du XVIᵉ siècle* (Limoges, 1943), p. 53. See also Robles, *Filósofos mexicanos del siglo XVI*, pp. 122–123.

61. John T. McNeill, *Modern Christian Movements* (Philadelphia, 1954), p. 34.

62. Saul K. Padover, *A Jefferson Profile* (New York, 1956), p. 344.

63. *Selected Writings of Bolívar*. Compiled by Vicente Lecuna, edited by Harold A. Bierck, Jr. (2 vols., New York, 1951), I, 119.

64. Toribio Esquivel Obregón, *El indio en la historia de México* (México, 1930). The material on this subject is extensive. During the Porfirio Díaz regime in Mexico, for example, the *científicos* followed the view that "Indians and mixed breeds were a pretty hopeless and dangerous lot, doomed by biology to inferiority and wardship", Howard F. Cline, *The United States and Mexico* (Cambridge—Mass., 1953), p. 55.

The Spanish feeling of superiority at the time of the conquest still exercises a profound influence on Mexican character, according to Leopoldo Zea, "Dialéctica de la conciencia de América", *Cuadernos Americanos*, año X, no. LVII (Mexico, 1951), 87–102. The many-volumed series on "México y lo Mexicano", directed by Zea, shows how wide-spread and diversified are the problems involved. For analyses of this problem, which is absorbing much time of the Mexican intellectuals, see Gordon W. Hewes, "Mexicans in Search of the 'Mexican'. Notes on Mexican National Character Studies", *The American Journal of Economics and Sociology*, XIII (New York, 1954), 209–223, and John Leddy Phelan, "México y lo mexicano", *Hispanic American Historical Review*, XXXVI (August, 1956), 309–318.

65. For an attack on these contemporary proponents of the inferiority of Indians, see Juan Comas, *Ensayos sobre indigenismo* (Mexico, 1953), pp. 26–51. A recent reference to Indian "inferiority" is in *América Indígena* (Mexico, 1956), no. 1, pp. 5–6.

66. Information supplied by Mr. Richard Patch, who spent the years 1953–1955 in Bolivia under the auspices of the Institute of Current World Affairs of New York. See his report dated August 6, 1955, on "Two Years of Agrarian Reform". Miguel Bonifaz, professor of

Derecho Indiano in the University of Sucre, has developed a Marxist interpretation of the history of Bolivia in which he applies the doctrine of Lenin and Stalin, but also recognizes that the theories of Las Casas and Sepúlveda have been involved, *El problema agrario-indígena en Bolivia* (Sucre, 1953), pp. 4–5. For other recent treatments of the position of the Bolivian Indians, see Abelardo Villalpando Retamozo, *La cuestión del indio* (Potosí, 1939), and Joaquín Villanueva Prado, "El 'Problema del indio', en Bolivia", *Cuadernos Hispanoamericanos*, XXIX (Madrid, 1956), no. 84, pp. 314–338.

67. Gottfried Handel, "Über die Einschätzung des Kolonialismus", *Wissenschaftliche Zeitschrift der Karl-Marx-Universität Leipzig*, 4 Jahrgang (1954/55). Gesellschaft-und-Sprachwissenschaftliche Reihe, heft 3/4, p. 389.

68. *Europe's Discovery of South Africa*, p. 256.

69. A. M. Ashley-Montague, *Statement on Race* (New York, 1951), p. 142.

APPENDIX A

1. Originally located in the Convento de San Felipe in Sucre, Bolivia, this volume of manuscripts was recently acquired by a bookdealer and then purchased by the Creole Foundation in Caracas for presentation to the Academia Nacional de la Historia there. For more information on how the letters were found, see Appendix B.

The dates of the letters are not given, but they were probably written while the discussions were being held in 1550–1551, or in the years immediately after the controversy. Sepúlveda refers to Castro's work *De iusta punitione haereticorum*, which was first published in 1547, and had a high opinion of Castro's learning as may be seen in Losada, *Sepúlveda a través de su "Epistolario"*, pp. 288–289. Castro had interested himself in the Valladolid dispute, for the San Felipe convent has a manuscript by him entitled "Resumen hecho por F. Alonso de Castro de la controversia habida entre Las Casas y el Dr. Sepúlveda y los pareceres de ambos sobre si es lícito a S. M. hacer la guerra a los indios y sujetarlos, para predicarles la fe". This *Resumen* is contained in the same volume as the letters, and probably was based on the résumé made by Domingo de Soto of the controversy and published by Las Casas in Seville in 1552.

2. Here are the pertinent sentences, as quoted by Olarte, *Alfonso de Castro*, pp. 263–265, 275: "Et testimonio hujus praecepti divini fretus, ego sentio justum esse bellum quod catholici Hispaniarum Reges contra barbaras gentes et idolatras, quae Deum ignorabant, versus Occidens et Austrum inventas ante aliquot annos, gesserunt et nunc etiam gerunt.

... Hanc autem monitionem oportet esse non levem et perfunctoriam quam facere solent homines in rebus parvi momenti, sed oportet esse monitionem vehementium et diligentium. .... Si autem tali admonitioni obtemperare noluerint, sed obstinati in suo errore perstiterint, praesertim si Dei verbi praedicationem impediant, tunc justum erit quod ob hanc causam, contra illos geratur bellum."

3. It is difficult for a non-theologian to understand this application of *correctio fraterna* to the waging of war against American Indians as a preliminary to their conversion, for it is defined as "une oeuvre de miséricorde, accomplie sous l'impulsion de la charité et la direction de la prudence", according to the *Dictionnaire de Théologie Catholique* ...., III, Part 2 (Paris, 1938), 1907.

It would seem that *correctio fraterna* is to be used only for the benefit of other Christians and, beginning with Christ, a number of important steps were set forth in some detail as the correct way to apply the doctrine. In certain cases, particularly when it was ascertained that secret admonitions would do no good, direct action is permitted (*ibid.*, pp. 1910–1911). But how could anyone be certain that private, peaceful persuasion would not work with the Indians unless it had first been tried? And it would appear that the doctrine could not be used on the Indians who had not previously known about Christianity, for the obligation to admonish one's neighbours "does not obtain, generally speaking, for the case of one who violates a law through invincible ignorance", *The Catholic Encyclopedia*, IV (New York, 1908), p. 394. *Correctio fraterna* is a fine phrase, in the same tradition as the 1573 law which substituted "pacification" for "conquest" to describe Spanish operations in America.

APPENDIX B

1. "Los archivos de la antigua Chuquisaca", *Boletín del Instituto de Investigaciones Históricas*, IX (Buenos Aires, 1929), 298–315. A list of the material appears on pp. 313–315.

2. *Las teorías políticas de Bartolomé de Las Casas* (Buenos Aires, 1935).

3. Printed, with an introduction by the writer, in "Un festón de documentos lascasianos", *Revista Cubana*, XVI (La Habana, julio-diciembre, 1941), 152–195.

4. The role of this episode in the long history of the disputes on Indian capacity has been described by the writer in *The First Social Experiments in America*, pp. 40–71.

INDEX

Acosta, José de, 56, 89, 90
Albornoz, Bartolomé de, 80
Alexander, 98
Alexander VI, 8, 16, 40, 64
Alfonso the Wise, 48
Alice's Adventures in Wonderland, 110
Altamira, Rafael, 48, 109
Anaya, Dr, 74
Andrada, Friar Rodrigo de, 29
Angostura Congress (1819), 114
Antonino, St, 61
Apartheid, 103
Aquinas, Thomas, 40
Araucanian Indians, 65
Archdale, John, 100
Arcos, Fray Miguel de, 79
Arévalo, Bernardino de, 38, 40, 79
Argüelles, Agustín de, 93
Aristotle, works: *Politics*, 31, 57, 59;
  Nicomachean Ethics, 56; theory of natural
  slavery, 14 ff., 44 ff.
Augustine, St, 3, 18, 52, 105
Averröes, 48

Bacon, Lord, 101
Bahia, 108
Baptismal methods, 21
Barbeyrac, 101
Barcelona, 16, 18
Bataillon, Marcel, 34
Bejarano, Lázaro, 80
Belgium, 45
Benavente, Toribio de (Motolinía), 21-22
Benzoni, Girolamo, 26
Bering Sea, 26
Beristain de Souza, José Mariano, 93
Betanzos, Domingo de, 23, 24
Bolívar, Simón, 114
Bolivia, 115
Bosphorus, 42
Bry, Theodore de, 26
Buenos Aires, 14

Cabral, Pedro Alvares, 107
Caesar, Julius, 68
Calvin, 99
Camels, 10
Canary Islands, 2

Cáncer, Luis, 67
Cano, Melchor, 31, 38, 74
Caribs, 18-19
Carmellones, Fernando de, 18
Casa del Montejo, 4
Castellanos, Juan de, 19
Castle of San Angelo, 46
Castro, Alfonso de, 60, 63, 65, 117-118
Castro, Américo, 37
Catherine of Medici, 51
Cervantes de Salazar, Francisco, 82
"Chantre de Chiapa", 84
Charles V, 10, 13, 16, 22, 34, 37, 38, 45,
  46, 47, 48, 56, 65, 72, 84, 96, 109
Chiapa, 28, 33
Chile, 84
Chiribiche, 66
Cieza de León, Pedro, 5
Claver, Pedro, 9
Clement VII, 45, 46, 50
Cole, S. G. and M. W., 103
Colegio de Santa Cruz, 56
Colegio de Tlatelolco, 19, 93
Columbus, 3, 50
Copán, 102
Copernicus, 12
Correctio fraterna, 64
Cortes of Cádiz, 93
Cortez, Ferdinand, 3, 5, 13, 47, 49, 50, 51,
  52, 53
Council of Castile, 31, 38
"Council of the Fourteen", 38
Council of the Indies, 29, 35, 36, 38, 49,
  51, 74, 89
Cuba, 19
Cuningham, William, 99

Darwin, 102
Deustúa, Alejandro O., 105
Diccionario de la lengua castellana, 59
Díaz del Castillo, Bernal, 49, 50, 52
Dürer, Albrecht, 49

Egyptians, 55, 98
El Dorado, 5
Encomienda, 60, 71, 72

Fabié, Antonio María, 94
Fernández de Navarrete, Domingo, 92
Fernández de Oviedo, Gonzalo, 4
Ferdinand and Isabella, 8, 10
Ferdinand the Catholic, 47
Ferrer, Juan, 23
Florida, 66
Fountain of Youth, 3
France, 45
Friede, Juan, 76, 105

Gálvez, Bernardo de, 112
Gandía, Enrique de, 106
Gasca, Pedro de la, 34–35
Gauls, 68
Gay Calbó, Enrique, 109
Ginés de Sepúlveda, Juan, works: *Against Those Who Depreciate or Contradict the Bull and Decree of Pope Alexander VI*, etc., 40; *Demócrates*, 43 ff., 62 ff.; *Here is contained a Dispute or Controversy*, etc., 76; *Rash, Scandalous and Heretical Propositions Which Dr. Sepúlveda Noted*, etc., 78; *Opera*, 43; correspondence with Alfonso de Castro, 60, 63, 65–66, 117–118
Gerbi, Antonello, 53
Germany, 45
Glidden, 102
Gog and Magog, 6
Golden Age, 20
Granada, 8
Gratiolet, 101
Great Khan, 20
Greeks, 55
Gregoire, Abbé, 93
Guerra, Balthasar, 30
Guzmán, Nuño de, 26

Hawaii, 101
Henry, Matthew, 114
Herodotus, 98
Herrera, Antonio de, 91
Herrera, Hernando de, 55
Hispaniola, 17
Holy Land, 69
Honduras, 14
Hunt, Dr, 101
Hurtado de Mendoza, Andrés, 83

Idolatry, 69
Inca culture, 49
Indians, attitudes towards, 6–7, 23–25, 46–48
Isabella, 8, 10
Isidore, 48
Israel, Ten Tribes of, 6
Italy, 58

James, St, Apostle, 5
Jefferson, Thomas, 114
Jerome, St, 50
John of Holywood, 4

Karl Marx University, 115
Kelemen, Pál, 52

Las Casas, Bartolomé de, works: *Apologetic History*, 54, 57; *Apologia*, 39, 42, 54; *Confesionario*, 28, 76; *History of the Indies*, 113–114; *The Only Way of Attracting All People to the True Religion*, 28, 42, 85; *Very Brief Account of the Destruction of the Indies*, 75
Law of 1573 on new discoveries, 86
Laws of Burgos, 15, 27, 41
Laws of the Indies, 110
Lawson, John, 100
Lizárraga, Reginaldo de, 85
Loaysa, Gerónimo de, 82, 83
Logan, Rayford W., 103
London, 64
López, Alonso, 89
López, Gregorio, 38, 75
López, Luis, 90
López, Tomás, 28
López de Gómara, Francisco, 3, 78
Losada, Ángel, 43, 67, 76
Lucan, 48
Lull, Ramón, 42
Luther, 20
Lutherans, 45

Major, John, 14, 64, 80
Maldonado, Alonso de, 31
Manila, 14, 109
Manzano y Manzano, Juan, 86, 87
Maracapana, 66
Mass baptism, 20
Matienzo, Juan de, 83
Maya culture, 49
Mendieta, Jerónimo de, 90
Menéndez y Pelayo, Marcelino, 94
Menéndez Pidal, Ramón, 95
Mesa de Conciencia, 108
Mexico, conquest of, 62
Mexico City, 29; Town Council of, 76, 82
Mier, Servando Teresa de, 93
Milan, 45
Monomotapa, Emperor of, 108
Montesinos, Antonio de, 14, 15
Montezuma, 47, 49
Moors, 97
More, Thomas, 78
Motolinía, *see* Benavente, Toribio de
Muñoz, Cristóbal, 10
Murray, Gilbert, 48

Naples, 45
Nebrija, Antonio de, 8, 59
Negro slavery, 9
Nehru, Jawaharlal, 103
New Hebrides, 101
New Laws, 29, 34, 72
Niebuhr, Reinhold, 104
Nordenskiöld, Erland, 53
Numantia, 48
Nunes, Leonard, 108
Núñez de Vela, Blasco, 34

Oaxaca, 22, 29
Orellana, Francisco de, 5
Orwell, George, 66, 105
Ovando, Juan de, 86

Palatino de Curzola, Vicente, 80
Paraguayan missions, 42
Paul III, 19, 21, 23, 84
Pauw, Cornelius de, 92, 93
Paz, Matías de, 15
Peña, Pedro de la, 80
Pérez de Castro, Juan, 81
Pérez de Oliva, Hernán, 56
Perpetuidad, 29
"Perro moro", 15
Persians, 98
Pharaoh, 35
Philip II, 29, 59, 64, 75, 83, 85
Philippines, 84
Phillips, Ulrich B., 102
Pigtails, 109
Pirito, 66
Pius IV, 84
Pius V, 84, 85
Pliny, 12
Pomponazzi, Pietro, 58
Puffendorf, 101

Queensland, 101
Quevedo, Bishop Juan, 16, 48
Quiñones, Cardinal Francisco de, 21
Quiroga, Pedro de, 85
Quiroga, Vasco de, 20, 78, 79

Ragatz, Lowell J., 104
Remesal, Antonio de, 33
René-Moreno, Gabriel, 102
Requirement, 16, 63, 86, 96
Ricard, Robert, 93
Romans, 55
Rome, Sack of, 45, 46
Romero, Francisco, 12
Rouen, 51

Sahagún, Bernardino de, 86
Salas, Manuel de, 93
Salmerón, Juan, 83
Sánchez, Alonso, 89
Sandoval, Alonso de, 9
San Gregorio monastery, 75
San Martín, the Liberator, 105
Santo Tomás, Domingo de, 23, 29, 105
Scythians, 46
Seagoing virgins, 3
Seneca, 48
Sigüenza, José de, 92
Silva, Juan de, 91
Simón, Pedro, 92
Solomons, 101
Solórzano Pereira, Juan de, 92
Sothos, 104
Soto, Domingo de, 27, 34, 38, 39, 42, 67, 74, 97, 107
Soto, Francisco de, 35
Spencer, Herbert, 102
Stephens, John L., 102
Strabo, 12

Tarn, 98
Tehuacán, 22
Tenamaztle, Don Francisco, 51
Ten Tribes of Israel, 6
Thomas, St, 105
Thorp, Captain George, 99
Tlaxcala, 4, 21
Toledo, Francisco de, 83
Town Council of Mexico, 76, 82
Tunis, 45
Tupinambas, 51

United Nations, 116
University of Alcalá, 22, 80, 89
    Mexico, 82
    Salamanca, 31, 89
    Seville, 111
Ursula, St, 3

Valdés, Alfonso de, 46
Valdivia, Pedro de, 65
Valencia, Martín de, 20
Valladolid, 23, 27, 28, 39, 50
Vargas Mexía, Francisco, 80
Vasconcelos, José, 106
Vázquez de Menchaca, Fernando, 81, 82
Velasco, Luis de, 30
Velázquez, Governor Diego, 5
Venezuela, 91
Vera Paz, 28–29, 33–34, 85
Vieira, Antonio, 108
Vitoria, Francisco de, 38, 64, 106, 107, 109

Wardell, Dr, 101
Welch, Sidney R., 115

Xenophon, 98
Xochimilco, 20

Yucatán, 55

Zorita, Alonso de, 50
Zulus, 104
Zumárraga, Juan de, 19, 24